THE PARDONER'S WALLET

The Pardoner's Wallet

BY SAMUEL McCHORD CROTHERS

Essay Index Reprint Series

BOOKS FOR LIBRARIES PRESS
FREEPORT, NEW YORK

First Published 1905
Reprinted 1972

Library of Congress Cataloging in Publication Data

Crothers, Samuel McChord, 1857-1927.
    The pardoner's wallet.

    (Essay index reprint series)
    Reprint of the 1905 ed.
    CONTENTS: The pardoner.--Unseasonable virtues.--
An hour with our prejudices. [etc.]
    I. Title.
PS3505.R9P3 1972   814'.5'2   78-39161
ISBN 0-8369-2685-4

PRINTED IN THE UNITED STATES OF AMERICA
BY
NEW WORLD BOOK MANUFACTURING CO., INC.
HALLANDALE, FLORIDA 33009

TO KATHARINE

WITH WHOM THESE THINGS HAVE
BEEN TALKED OVER

PREFACE

THERE is a well-grounded prejudice against a volume which exhibits no marks of design and which turns out to be only a fortuitous collection of essays. It is felt that the chapters brought together under the cover of a single book should have something in common. When one sees a number of subjects, each standing aloof from the others, he predicts infelicity. It suggests incompatibility of temper.

The essays brought together in " the Pardoner's Wallet" have at least a certain community of interest. They treat of aspects of human nature which, while open to friendly criticism, are excusable. If the author sometimes touches upon the foibles of his betters, he at least has the grace to know that they are his betters.

CONTENTS

THE PARDONER

With him ther rood a gentil Pardoner
Of Rouncival, his freend and his compeer,
That streight was comen fro the Court of Rome.
. . . .

A vernicle hadde he sowed on his cappe
His walet lay biforn him in his lappe
Bretful of pardoun.

I HAVE no plea to make for this fourteenth-century pardoner. He was an impudent vagabond, trafficking in damaged goods. One did not need to be a Lollard in order to see that he was a reprehensible character. Discerning persons in need of relics would go to responsible dealers where they could be assured of getting their money's worth. This glib-tongued fellow peddling religious articles from door to door lived on the credulity of untraveled country people. He took advantage of their weaknesses. Many a good wife would purchase a pardon she had no need of, simply because he offered it as a

bargain. This was all wrong. We all know how
the business of indulgence-selling was overdone.
There was a general loss of confidence on the
part of the purchasing public ; and at last in the
days of the too enterprising Tetzel there came a
disastrous slump.   There was no market for pardons, even of the gilt-edged varieties.   Since then
very little has been doing in this line, at least
among the northern nations.

The pardoner richly deserved his fate. And yet
there are times when one would give something
to see the merry knave coming down the road.

I suppose that the nature of each individual
has its point of moral saturation.   When this
point is reached, it is of no use to continue exhor-
tation or rebuke or any kind of didactic effort.
Even the finest quality of righteous indignation
will no longer soak in.   With me the point
of moral saturation comes when I attend suc-
cessively more meetings of a reformatory and
denunciatory character than nature intended me
to profit by.   If they are well distributed in point
of time, I can take in a considerable number of
good causes and earnestly reprobate an equal
number of crying evils.   But there is a certain

monotony of rebuke which I am sure is not bene-
ficial to persons of my disposition. That some
things are wrong I admit, but when I am
peremptorily ordered to believe that everything
is wrong, it arouses in me a certain obstinacy of
contradiction. I might be led to such a belief, but
I will not be driven to it. I rebel against those
censors of manners and morals who treat all human imperfectnesses with equal rigor. To relax
even for an instant the righteous frown over the
things that are going wrong, into an indulgent
smile at the things that are not nearly so bad as
they seem, is in their eyes nothing less than com-
pounding a felony. If they would allow proper
intervals between protests, so that the conscience
could cool down, all would be well. But this is
just what they will not allow. The wheels must
go round without intermission until progress is
stopped by the disagreeable accident of "a hot
box."

You remember after Mrs. Proudie had given
her guests a severe lesson in social ethics, the Sig-
nora asked in her hearing, —

" ' Is she always like this ? '

" ' Yes — always — madam,' said Mrs. Proudie,

returning; 'always the same — always equally adverse to impropriety of conduct of every description.'"

Mrs. Proudie was an excellent woman according to her light, yet Barchester would have been a happier place to live in had her light been less constant. A little flicker now and then, a momentary relief from the glare, would have been appreciated.

It is when the note of personal responsibility has been forced beyond my ability that I feel beneath my inherited Puritanism the stirring of a vague Papistry. Instead of joining another protesting society beginning with that feverish particle "anti," how delightful it would be to go out and dicker with a well-conditioned pardoner

        Streight comen fro the Court of Rome!

Wearied with diatribes and resolutions, one falls back upon the guileless bargainings of Simple Simon.

"Let me taste your ware," say I.

"Show me first your penny," says the pardoner.

There is a renewal of one's youth in this immortal repartee.

There is no greater relief than to go out and

buy something, especially if one can buy it cheap.
A great part of the attractiveness of the mediæval
indulgences lay in the fact that you could buy
them. They would not have seemed the same
if they had been given away, or if you had to work
them out like a road tax. To go out and buy a
little heart's ease was an enticement.

Then again, the natural man, when he has to
do with an institution, is in a passive rather than
in an active mood. If it is instituted for his bet-
terment, he says, " Let it better me." It seems
too bad that in the end it should throw all the
responsibility back upon himself.

A delightful old English traveler criticises the
methods of transportation he found in vogue in
parts of Germany. He says that on the Rhine
it was customary to make the passengers do the
rowing. " Their custome is that the passengers
must exercise themselves with oares and rowing,
alternis vicibus, a couple together. So that the
master of the boate (who methinks in honestie
ought either to do it himself or to procure some
others to do it for him) never roweth but when
his turne commeth. This exercise both for recreation and health sake is I confesse very convenient

for man. But to be tied unto it by way of strict necessitie when one payeth well for his passage was a thing that did not a little distaste my humour."

This is the trouble which many of us find in the modern methods of doing good. There are all sorts of organizations which promise well. But no sooner have we embarked on a worthy undertaking than we find that we are expected to work our passage. The officers of the boat disclaim all further responsibility, leaving that to private judgment. It is the true Protestant way and it works excellently well, when it works at all. It offers a fine challenge to disinterested virtue. But there are occasions when the natural man rebels. To have so much put upon him doth "not a little distaste his humour." He longs for the good old times when there were thinkers who were not above their business, and who when he was at his wit's end would do his thinking for him. It's the same way with being excused for his shortcomings. Of course on a pinch he can excuse himself, but he generally makes a pretty poor job of it. It would be much more satisfactory to have a duly authorized person who, for a consideration, would assume the whole responsibility. Of course if he had done something that was really unpardonable, that would be another matter. The law would have to take its course. But there are a great many venial transgressions. What he wants is some one who can assure him that they are venial.

Let no good Protestant take offense at the finding of a Pardoner's Wallet in this twentieth century. It is only a wallet containing tentative suggestions concerning things pardonable. Nothing is authoritatively signed and sealed.

Of one thing let the good Protestant take notice. I would have my pardoner know his place. He must not meddle with things too high for him. He has no right to deal with the graver sins or to speak for a higher power. He must not speak even in the name of the Church, which has worthier spokesmen than he. In a book on indulgences the author says, "On the subject of elongated, centenary, and millenary pardons, it would take too much space to enlarge." I should rule out all such ambitious plans, not only from lack of space but on conscientious grounds.

My pardoner should confine himself to a more

modest task. He should be the spokesman not of any ecclesiastical power, but only of ordinary and errant human nature. There are sins against eternal law that must at all times be taken seriously. The trouble with us poor mortals is that, even in our remorse, we do not take very long views. The judgment that seems most terrible to us is that of the people who live next door. The transgressions which loom largest are offenses against social conventions and against our own sensitive vanity. The pangs of remorse for an act of remembered awkwardness are likely to be more poignant than those which come as retribution for an acknowledged crime.

Here is ample room for a present-day pardoner. I should like to hear him make the cheery proclamation of his trade.

"Good friends: You are not what you would like to be. You are not what you think you are. You are not what your neighbors think you are, — or rather, you are not what you think your neighbors think you are. Your foibles, your peccadillos, your fallacies, and your prejudices are more numerous than you imagine. But take heart of grace, good people. These things are not unpardonable. We indulgencers have learned to make allowances for human nature. Let's see what's in my wallet! No crowding! Each will be served in his turn."

If I were a duly licensed pardoner, I should have a number of nicely engraved indulgences for what are called sins of omission. Not that I should attempt to extenuate the graver sort. I should not hold out false hopes to thankless sons or indifferent husbands. To be followed by such riff-raff would spoil my trade with the better classes. I should not have anything in my wallet for the acrimonious critic, who brings a railing accusation against his neighbor, and omits to sign his name. Some omissions are unpardonable.

I should, at the beginning, confine my traffic to those sins which easily beset conscientious persons about half past two in the morning. We have warrant for thinking that the sleep of the just is refreshing. This is doubtless true of the completely just; but with the just man in the making it is frequently otherwise. There is a stage in his strenuous moral career which is conducive to insomnia.

Having gone to sleep because he was tired, he presently awakes for the same reason. He is, however, only half awake. Those kindly comforters, Common-sense, Humor, and Self-esteem, whose function it is to keep him on reasonably good terms with himself while he is doing his necessary work, are still dozing.

Then Conscience appears, — a terrible apparition. There is a vague menace in her glance. The poor wretch cowers beneath it. Then is unrolled the lengthening list of the things left undone which ought to have been done. Every unwritten letter and uncalled call and unattended committee meeting and unread report emerges from the vasty deep and adds its burden of unutterable guilt. The Thing That Was Not Worth Doing arises and demands with insatiate energy that it be done at once. The Thing Half-done, because there was no time to finish it, appears with wan face accusing him of its untimely taking off. The Stitch not Taken in Time appears with its pitiful ninefold progeny all doomed because of a moment's inattention. It seems that his moral raiment, instead of being put together with an eye to permanency, has been stitched on a single-thread machine and the end of the seam never properly fastened. Now he is pulling at the thread, and he sees the whole fabric unraveling before his eyes.

His past existence looms before him as a battlefield with a perpetual conflict of duties, — each duty cruelly slain by its brother duty. While the wailing of these poor ghosts is in his ears he cannot rest. And yet he knows full well that at half past two in the morning the one inexorable duty is that he should go to sleep. Conscience points to this as another duty left undone. Then begins a new cycle of self-reproach.

At such times the sight of an indulgence neatly framed hanging upon the bedroom wall would be worth more than it would cost. It would save doctor's bills.

Even in our waking hours there is a tendency for the sins of omission and the sorrows of omission to pile up in monstrous fashion. There is a curious ingenuity which some persons have in loading themselves with burdens which do not belong to them, and in extracting melancholy reflections out of their good fortune. They will not frankly accept a blessing in its own proper form,

— it must come to them in a mournful disguise.
Poets seem particularly subject to these inversions
of feeling. Here are some lines entitled "Two
Sorrows:" —

> Before Love came my eyes were dim with tears
>   Because I had not known her gentle face.
> Softly I said, "But when across the years
>   Her smile illumes the darkness of my place,
>   All grief from my poor heart she will efface."
>
> Now Love is mine — she walks with me for aye
>   Down paths of primrose and blue violet,
> But on my heart at every close of day
>   A grief more keen than my old grief is set.
>   I weep for those who have not found Love yet.

There is a fine altruism about this sentiment
that one cannot but respect; yet I should hate to
live with a person who felt that way. One would
not venture on any little kindness for fear of opening a new floodgate of tears.

I should feel like urging another point of view.
It is true that you are happy, happier than you
deserve. But don't get morbid about it; take it
cheerfully. It's not your fault. It seems selfish,
you say, to enjoy your blessings when there are n't
enough to go round among all your fellow beings.

Why, my dear fellow, that's the only way to make them go around. What if, theoretically, it is a little selfish? We will readily pardon that for the sake of the satisfaction we get out of seeing you have a good time. We much prefer that you should allow us to sympathize with you in your happiness, rather than that you should inflict upon us too much sympathy for our deprivations.

There is opportunity for a thriving trade in indulgences for necessarily slighted work. I emphasize the idea of necessity, for I am aware of the danger of gross abuse if poets and painters should get the notion that they may find easy absolution for the sin of offering to the public something less than their best. Their best is none too good. We must not, through misdirected charity, lower the standards of self-respecting artists.

But some of us are not artists. The ordinary man is compelled to spend most of his time on pot-boilers of one kind or another. When the pot is merrily boiling, and all the odds and ends are being mingled in a savory stew, I would allow the ordinary man some satisfaction. As fingers were made before forks, so mediocrity was made before genius. Has mediocrity no right to enjoy its own work, just because it is not the very best ?

We of the commonalty who are fitted to live happily in the comparative degree, allow ourselves to be bullied by the superlative. There are uneasy spirits who trouble Israel. They continually quote the maxim that whatever is worth doing is worth doing well. It is a good maxim in its way, and causes no particular hardship until our eyes are opened and we see what it means to do anything superlatively well. When we are shown by example the technical excellence which is possible in the simplest forms of activity, and the extent to which we fall short, we are appalled. It is a wonder that we keep going at all when we consider the slovenly way we breathe. And yet breathing, though it well might engage all our attention, is only one of the things we have to do.

I attribute a good deal of the sense of stress in modern life to the new standards of excellence that are set in regard to the multifarious activities which make up our daily lives. We have to do a hundred different things. This is not particularly trying so long as it is merely touch and go. In our amateurish way we rather enjoy the variety. But when a hundred experts beset us, each one of whom has made a life study of a particular act, we are bowed in contrition. There is no good in us but good intentions, and they cannot save us. Our life story is summed up like that of the unfortunate sparrow in the tragical history of Cock Robin:

His aim then he took
But he took it not right.

Our capacity for imperfectness seems absolutely unlimited. The effort taken to achieve success in one direction is from another point of view a dissipation of energy. It is so much power withdrawn from another possible achievement. The most versatile men do not do all things equally well, and while the world calls them successful they are inwardly conscious of their manifold failures. Mr. Balfour as Prime Minister of the British Empire has had much to gratify his ambition, but he takes the public into his confidence and confesses that he is a bitterly disappointed man.

For, in addition to other accomplishments, he plays golf, a game that develops a conscience of its own. He plays well, but his conscience tells him that he does not play as well as he might. " I belong," he says, " to that unhappy class of beings forever pursued by remorse, who are conscious that they threw away in youth opportunities that were open to them of beginning golf at a time of life when alone the muscles can be attuned to the full perfection required by the most difficult game that perhaps exists."

Surely there must be a way by which such vain regrets may be stilled. Life has its inevitable compromises. We cannot always be at our best. Take such a simple matter as that of masticating our food. Before I had given much thought to it, I should have said that it was something worth doing and worth doing well. When I learned that Mr. Gladstone was accustomed to chew each morsel of food thirty-two times, I thought it greatly to his credit. For a man who had so many other things to do, that seemed enough.

But when I read a book of some three hundred pages containing the whole duty of man in regard to chewing, I was disheartened. Mr. Gladstone appeared to be a mere tyro guilty of bolting his food. " The author has found that one fifth of the midway section of the garden young onion, sometimes called shallot, has required seven hundred and twenty-two mastications before disappearing through involuntary swallowing."

The author evidently did his whole duty by that young onion, and yet I should have pardoned him if he had done something less. That doctrine of his about involuntary swallowing being the only kind that is morally justifiable, seems to me to be too austere. If we have to swallow in the end, why not show a cheerful willingness?

Not only do those need comfort who do less than is expected of them, those who do more are often in an equally sorry plight. Their excellences make them obnoxious to their neighbors, and are treated as unpardonable offenses. I would have a special line of indulgences for that class of people known as the " unco guid." I know no persons more in need of charity, and who get so little of it. Every man's hand is against them, especially every hand that wields the pen of a ready writer. They seem predestinated to literary reprobation, and that without regard to their genuinely good works or to their continuance in the same. And yet the whole extent of their crime is that, being in some respects better than their neighbors, they are painfully aware of the fact. It is because they have tasted of the forbidden knowledge of their own moral superiority that their fall is deemed irremediable.

I confess that, in spite of all that has been said against them, I have a tender feeling for them. They are persecuted for self-righteousness without the benefit of any beatitude. Why should we consider it unpardonable to be fully cognizant of one's undoubted virtues? Of course unconscious virtue is the more paradisiacal, while conscious virtue often rubs one the wrong way. But while there are so many worse things in the world, why should we mind a little thing like that?

We listen to Dumas' swashbuckling heroes recounting their transgressions. We know that they are not so bad as they would have us believe, but we think no worse of them for that. But let a thoroughly respectable man draw attention to his own fine qualities, and we treat every deviation from exact fact as a crime. When he indulges in some exaggeration and pictures himself as rather better than he is, we cry, "Hypocrite!" If he claims possession of some single virtue which does not, in our judgment, harmonize with some of his other characteristics, we treat him as if he had stolen it. And yet, poor fellow! he may have come honestly by this bit of finery, though he has not been able to get other things to match it. All this is unkind.

Whatever one may think of the "unco guid," every right-minded person must agree with me that something ought to be done for the peace of mind of the quiet, respectable, good people who bear the heat and burden of the day. I have in mind the people who pay taxes, and build homes, and support churches and schools and hospitals, and now and then go to the theatre. They are as likely as not to be moderately well to do, and if they are not, nobody knows it. When times are hard with them, they keep their own counsels and go about with head erect and the best foot forward. You may see multitudes of these people every day.

As a class, these people are sadly put upon. They are criticised not only for their own short-

comings, but for those of all their irresponsible
fellow citizens. If anything goes wrong they are
sure to hear about it, for they listen to sermons,
and read the newspapers, and attend meetings.
No reformer can be truly eloquent who does not
point his finger at his hearer, and say, "Thou art
the man!" Now, unfortunately, the real delin-
quents are usually absent, and the right-minded,
conscientious hearer of the word, who is doing
all he can for social regeneration, even to the verge
of nervous prostration, has to act as substitute.
He has been so often assured that he is the guilty
man that, by and by, he comes to believe it.

He walks to church with his family only to be
told that it is his fault, and the fault of those like
him, that other people have gone off in their
automobiles. Perhaps, if he had walked differently, he might have made church-going more
attractive to them. The evils of intemperance
are laid at his door. It is not worth while to blame
the drunkard or the saloon-keeper; they are not
within ear-shot. As to pauperism and vice, every
one knows that they arise from social conditions;
and pray who is responsible for these conditions
unless it be the meek man who sits in the pew, —

at least, he is the only one who can readily be made to assume the responsibility.

There is something wholesome in all this if it be not overdone. I, myself, like to have my fling at the man who is trying to do his duty, and to twit him occasionally for not doing more. It keeps him from self-righteousness. But sometimes it is carried too far, and the poor man staggers under a load of vicarious guilt.

I especially hate to see the man who is trying to do his duty given over to the censures of those who do not try. There is something very harsh in the judgment of the ne'er-do-well upon his well-to-do brother. His attitude is the extreme of phariseeism, as he contrasts his own generous and care-free nature with the picayunish prudence which he scorns. To be sure, his brother in the end pays his debts for him, but he does it with a narrow scrutiny which robs the act of its natural charm. His acts of helpfulness are marred by a tendency to didacticism. All these things are laid up against him.

But allowance should be made for the difference in condition. Ne'er-do-wellness is an expansive state. There are no natural limits to it. It develops broad views, and its peculiar virtues have a free field. It is different with well-to-doness, which is a precarious condition with a very narrow margin of safety. The ne'er-do-well can afford to be generous, seeing that his generosity costs him nothing. He is free from all belittling calculations necessary to those who are compelled to adjust means to ends, — he is indifferent to ends and he has no means.

When the morally responsible person finds himself too much put upon, I would grant him a generous indulgence. After all, I would tell him, the prudential virtues are not so bad. It is a good deal of an achievement to make both ends meet. I am not disposed to be too hard on those who accomplish this, even though I may think a little fullness in their moral garments might be more becoming.

I should also make provision for the pardon of those good people who are harshly judged because their virtues are unseasonable. But their case involves delicate considerations that can best be treated in another chapter.

UNSEASONABLE VIRTUES

❧❧

THERE are certain philosophers who have fallen into the habit of speaking slightingly of Time and Space. Time, they say, is only a poor concept of ours corresponding to no ultimate reality, and Space is little better. They are merely mental receptacles into which we put our sensations. We are assured that could we get at the right point of view we should see that real existence is timeless. Of course we cannot get at the right point of view, but that does not matter.

It is easy to understand how philosophers can talk in that way, for familiarity with great subjects breeds contempt; but we of the laity cannot dismiss either Time or Space so cavalierly. Having once acquired the time-habit, it is difficult to see how we could live without it. We are accustomed to use the minutes and hours as stepping-stones, and we pick our way from one to

another. If it were not for them, we should find
ourselves at once beyond our depth. It is the
succession of events which makes them interesting. There is a delightful transitoriness about
everything, and yet the sense that there is more
where it all comes from. To the unsophisticated
mind Eternity is not the negation of Time; it is
having all the time one wants. And why may
not the unsophisticated mind be as nearly right in
such matters as any other?

In a timeless existence there would be no distinction between now and then, before and after.
Yesterdays and to-days would be merged in one
featureless Forever. When we met one another it
would be impertinent to ask, " How do you do?"
The chilling answer would be: "I do not do; I
am." There would be nothing more to say to one
who had reduced his being to such bare metaphysical first principles.

I much prefer living in Time, where there are
circumstances and incidents to give variety to
existence. There is a dramatic instinct in all of
us that must be satisfied. We watch with keen
interest for what is coming next. We would
rather have long waits than to have no shifting

of the scenes, and all the actors on the stage at once, doing nothing.

An open-minded editor prints the following question from an anxious reader in regard to a serial story appearing in his paper: "Does it make any difference in reading the serial whether I begin with Saturday's chapter and read backward toward Monday, or should the tale be read as the chapters appear?"

The editor assures his subscriber that the story is of such uniform excellence that it would read well in either direction. In practical affairs our dramatic instinct will not allow us this latitude. We insist upon certain sequences. There is an expectancy that one thing will lead up to another. We do not take kindly to an anti-climax or to an anachronism. The Hebrew sage declares, "He hath made everything beautiful in his time." That is in the right time, but alas for the beautiful thing that falls upon the wrong time! It is bewitched beyond all recognition by the old necromancer who has power to make "ancient good uncouth."

It is just here that charity requires that we should discriminate. There is a situation that de-

mands the services of a kind-hearted indulgencer.
Ethics has to do with two kinds of offenses: one
is against the eternal and unchanging standards
of right and wrong, and the other against the
perpetually varying conditions of the passing day.
We are continually confusing the two. We visit
upon the ancient uncouth good which comes
honestly stumbling on its belated journey toward
the perfect, all the condemnation that properly
belongs to willful evil. It is lucky if it gets off so
easily as that, for we are likely to add the pains
and penalties which belong to hypocritical pre-
tense. As for a premature kind of goodness coming before there is time properly to classify it, that
must expect martyrdom. Something of the old
feeling about strangers still survives in us. We
think it safer to treat the stranger as an enemy.
If he survives our attacks we may make friends
with him.

Those good people who, in their devotion to
their own ideals, have ignored all considerations
of timeliness, have usually passed through sore
tribulations. They have been the victims of cruel
misunderstandings. Such, for example, was Saint
Cerbonius. Cerbonius is one of the October saints.

October is a good month for saints. The ecclesiastical calendar gives us a sense of spiritual mellowness and fruitfulness. The virtues celebrated are without the acidity which belongs to some other seasons: witness Saint Francis of Assisi, Saint Teresa, Saint Luke, the beloved physician, Saint John Capistran, of whom it is written, " he had a singular talent for reconciling inveterate enemies and inducing them to love one another." Cerbonius has a modest place in this autumnal brotherhood; indeed, in some Lives of the Saints, he is not even mentioned, and yet he had the true October spirit. Nevertheless, his good was evil spoken of, and he came near to excommunication, and all because of his divergence from popular custom in the matter of time.

It seems that he lived towards the end of the sixth century, and that he was bishop of Piombino. Very soon a great scandal arose, for it was declared that the bishop was neglecting his duties. At the accustomed hour the citizens came to the cathedral for their devotions, only to find the chancel devoid of clergy. Cerbonius and his priests were at that moment comfortably seated at breakfast. Each succeeding morning witnessed the same scene. The bishop was evidently an infidel scoffing at the rites of religion. Appeal was made to Rome, and legates were appointed who confirmed the astounding rumors. At last Cerbonius went to Rome to plead his cause; but only by a special miracle was his character cleared. The miracle induced the authorities to look into the matter more carefully, and it was found that Cerbonius, instead of neglecting his duties, had been carried away by holy zeal. While the people of Piombino were still in their beds, Cerbonius and his clergy would be celebrating mass. As for breakfast, that was quite late in the day.

It is easy to be wise after the event, and now that the matter has been cleared up it is evident that all the religion was not on one side. Taking a large view of the subject, we see that in the course of the twenty-four hours the bishop spent as much time in the church as the most scrupulous parishioner could ask. But it was just this large view that they were unwilling to take. With them it was now or never. They judged his character by the cross-section which they took at one particular hour.

I suppose that, had I lived in Piombino, I

should have been a moderate anti-Cerbonian.
Cerbonius was in error, but not in mortal sin. He
was guilty of a heresy that disturbed the peace
of the church, — that of early rising. So long as
early rising is held only as a creed for substance
of doctrine and set forth as a counsel of perfection,
it may be tolerated, but when the creed becomes
a deed it awakens fanatical opposition. This
breeds schism. A person cannot be popular who
gets the reputation of being a human alarm clock.
The primitive instinct in regard to an alarm clock
is to stop it. If Cerbonius had possessed the tact
necessary to a man in his position, he would not
only have done his duty, but he would have done
it at the time most convenient to the greatest
number. His virtue was unseasonable; but between a man of unseasonable virtue and an aban-
doned character who has no virtue at all, there is
a great difference. It is just this difference which
the majority of people will not see. They make
no distinction between one who deliberately of-
fends against the eternal verities and one who
accidentally tramples upon a temporary verity
that he did n't know was there.

Most of our quarrels do not concern absolute

right and wrong; they arise from disputes about the time of day. Two persons may have the same qualities and convictions and yet never agree. An ironical fate sets them at cross purposes and they never meet without irritating contradictions. It is all because their moods do not synchronize. One is always a little too slow, the other a little too fast. When one is in fine fettle the other is just beginning to get tired. They are equally serious, but never on the same occasion, and so each accuses the other of heartless frivolity. They have an equal appreciation of a pleasantry, but they never see it at the same instant. One gives it an uproarious welcome when the other is speeding the parting guest.

Two quick-tempered people may live together very comfortably so long as they lose their tempers simultaneously; they are then ready to make up at the same time. They get on like an automobile, by a series of small explosions accurately timed. But when a quick-tempered person is unequally yoked with one who is slow to wrath, the case is difficult. The slowness causes continual apprehension. The fuse burns so deliberately that it seems to have gone out and then the explo-

sion comes. In such cases there can be no ade-
quate explanation. The offender would apologize
if he could remember what the offense was, and
he does n't dare to ask.

Said one theologian to another: "The difference between us is that your God is my Devil."
This involved more than the mere matter of nomenclature. It upset the spiritual time-table and
caused disastrous collisions. When one good man
set forth valiantly to fight the Devil, the other
would charge him with disturbing his worship.

The fact that one man's work is another man's
play is equally fruitful in misunderstandings. The
proverbial irritability of the literary and artistic
tribes arises in part from this cause. They feel that
they are never taken seriously. When we go to
a good play we find it so easy to be amused that
we do not realize what hard work it is for those
whose business it is to be amusing. The better
the work, the more effortless it seems to us. On
a summer afternoon we take up a novel in a mood
which to the conscientious novelist seems sacri-
lege. He has thrown all the earnestness of his
nature into it, and he wants his message to be
received in the same spirit. We have earnestness

of nature too, but we have expended it in other directions. Having finished our work, we take our rest by reading his. It is a pleasant way to pass the time. This enrages the novelist, and he writes essays to rebuke us. He calls us Philistines and other hard names, and says that we are incapable of appreciating literary art.

But what is our offense? We have used his work for our own purpose, which was to rest our minds. We got out of it what at the time we needed. Does he not act in very much the same way? Did we not see him at the town-meeting when a very serious question concerning the management of the town poor-house was to be settled? It was a time when every good citizen should have shown his interest by speaking an earnest word. Unmindful of all this, he sat through the meeting with the air of an amused outsider. He paid little attention to the weighty arguments of the selectmen, but noted down all their slips in grammar. He confessed unblushingly that he attended the meeting simply to get a little local color. What is to become of the country when a tax-payer will take the duties of citizenship so lightly?

These recriminations go on endlessly. Because we do not see certain qualities in action, we deny their existence. The owl has a reputation for sedentary habits and unpractical wisdom, simply because he keeps different business hours from those to which we are accustomed. Could we look in on him during the rush time, we would find him a hustling fellow. He has no time to waste on unremunerative meditation. This is his busy night. How ridiculous is the sleepiness of the greater part of the animal world! There is the lark nodding for hours on his perch. They say he never really wakes up — at least, nobody has seen him awake.

There is a pedagogical theory according to which each individual in his early life repeats quite accurately the history of mankind up to date. He passes through all the successive stages in the history of the race, with a few extra flourishes now and then to indicate the surprises which the future may have in store for us. The history of civilization becomes, for the initiated, the rehearsal of the intensely interesting drama of the nursery and the schoolroom. It lacks the delicacy of the finished performance, but it presents the argument clearly enough and suggests the necessary stage business. The young lady who attempts to guide a group of reluctant young cave-dwellers from one period in human culture to another is not surprised at any of their tantrums. Her only anxiety is lest some form of barbarism appropriate to their condition may have been skipped. Her chief function is like that of the chorus in the Greek tragedy, to explain to the audience each dramatic situation as it unfolds.

I should not like to take the responsibility of running such an excellent theory into the ground, yet it does seem to me that it might be carried further. Granted that childhood is innocent savagery and that adolescence is gloriously barbaric, what is the matter with mature life? Does it not have any remnants of primitiveness? Does not Tennyson write of " the gray barbarian " ?

The transitions from primitive savagery to civilization which took the race centuries to accomplish are repeated by the individual, not once but many times. After we get the knack of it, we can run over the alphabet of human progress backwards as well as forwards.

Exit Troglodyte. Enter Philosopher discoursing on disinterested virtue. Reënter Troglodyte. Such dramatic transformations may be expected by merely changing the subject of the conversation.

I remember sitting, one Sunday afternoon, on a vine-covered piazza reading to a thoughtful and irascible friend. The book was Martineau's "Endeavors after the Christian Life." In the middle of the second discourse my friend's dog rushed into the street to attack the dog of a passer-by. It was one of those sudden and unpredictable antipathies to which the members of the canine race are subject. My friend, instead of preserving a dignified neutrality, rushed into the fray in the spirit of offensive partisanship, and instantly became involved in an altercation with the gentleman on the sidewalk. Canes were brandished, fierce threats were exchanged, and only by the greatest efforts were the Homeric heroes separated. Returning to his chair, my friend handed me the book, saying, "Now let us go on with our religion." The religion went on as placidly as aforetime. There was no sense of confusion. The wrath of Achilles did not dis-

turb the calm spirituality of Martineau. Each
held the centre of the stage for his own moment,
and there was no troublesome attempt to harmonize them. Why should there be? Martineau was not talking about dogs.

I know no greater luxury than that of thinking well of my fellow-men. It is a luxury which
a person in narrow circumstances, who is compelled to live within the limits of strict veracity,
sometimes feels to be beyond his means. Yet I
think it no harm to indulge in a little extravagance in this direction. The best device for seeing all sorts and conditions of men to advantage
is to arrange them in their proper chronological
order.

For years it was the custom to speak dispar-
agingly of the "poor whites" of our Southern
mountains. Shut off from the main currents of
modern life, they seemed unpardonably unpro-
gressive. They were treated as mere degenerates.
At last, however, a keener and kindlier observer
hit upon a happy phrase. These isolated moun-
taineers, he said, have retained the characteristic
habits of a former generation. They are our "contemporary ancestors." Instantly everything was

put in a more favorable light; for we all are disposed to see the good points in our ancestors.
After all, the whole offense with which these
mountain people are charged is that they are behind the times. In our bona-fide contemporaries
this is a grave fault, but in our ancestors it is pardonable. We do not expect them to live up to
our standards, and so we give them credit for living up to their own.

In this case we agree to consider fifty miles of
mountain roads, if they be sufficiently bad, as the
equivalent of rather more than a hundred years
of time. Behind the barrier the twentieth century
does not yet exist. Many things may still be
winked at for which the later generation may be
sternly called to repentance. Then, too, the end
of the eighteenth century has some good points
of its own. These contemporary ancestors of ours
are of good old English stock, and we begin to
look upon them with a good deal of family
pride.

But when we once accept poor roads as the
equivalent of the passage of time, putting people
at the other end into another generation, there is
no knowing what we may come to in our chari-

table interpretations. For there are other equally effective non-conductors of thought. By the simple device of not knowing how to read, a man cuts off some thousands of culture years and saves himself from no end of intellectual distractions. He becomes the contemporary of " earth's vigorous, primitive sons." If to his illiteracy he adds native talent and imagination, there is a chance for him to make for himself some of those fine old discoveries which we lose because we got the answer from some blabbing book before we had come to the point of asking the question. Of course the danger is that if he has native talent and imagination he will learn to read, and it must be confessed that for this reason we do not get such a high order of illiterates as formerly.

I once made the acquaintance of an ancient Philosopher. His talents were for cosmogony, and his equipment would have been deemed ample in the days when cosmogony was the fashion. He had meditated much on the genesis of things and had read nothing, so that his speculations were uncontaminated by the investigations of others. He was just the man to construct a perfectly simple and logical theory of the universe, and he did it.

His universe was not like that of which our sciences give us imperfect glimpses, but it was very satisfactory to him. He was very fair in dealing with facts; he explained all that could be explained by his system. As the only criterion of a fact which he recognized was that it agreed with his system, there was none left over to trouble him. His manner of thought was so foreign to that of our time that his intellectual ability was not widely appreciated; yet had his birth not been so long delayed, he might have been the founder of a school and have had books written about him. For so far as I could learn, his views of the four elements of earth, air, fire, and water, were very much like those of the early Greek physicists. Had I taken him as a fellow American, I should have dismissed him as not up to date; but considering him in the light of an ancient sage, I found much in him to admire.

Once upon the coast of Maine I came upon a huge wooden cylinder. Within it was a smaller one, and in the centre, seated upon a swinging platform, was the owner of the curious contrivance. He was a mild-eyed, pleasant-spoken man, whom it was a pleasure to meet. He explained that this

was "The Amphibious Vehicle," and that it
would move equally well on land or sea.

"You know," said he, "what the prophet Ezekiel said about the 'wheel in the middle of a
wheel'?"

"Yes," I answered.

"Well, this is it."

There was something convincing in this matter-of-fact statement. The "wheel within a wheel"
had been to me little more than a figure of speech,
but here it was made out of good pine lumber,
with a plank in the middle for the living creature to sit on. It was as if I had fallen through
a trap door into another age. Here was a literal-
minded contemporary of Ezekiel, who, having
heard of the wheel within a wheel, had proceeded
at once to make one. I ascended into the precarious seat, and we conversed upon the spiritual
and temporal possibilities of the vehicle. I found
that on the scriptural argument he was clearly
ahead of me, being able to quote chapter and
verse with precision, while my references were
rather vague. In the field of mechanics he was
also my superior. I could not have made the
vehicle, having not yet emerged beyond the stone

age. As we talked I forgot that we were at the mouth of the Penobscot. We were on the "river of Chebar," and there was no knowing what might happen.

The belated philosophers and inventors, who think the thoughts of the ancient worthies after them, live peaceful lives. What matters it that they are separated by a millennium or two from the society in which they were fitted to shine? They are self-sufficing, and there are few who care to contradict them. It is not so with one who is morally belated. There is something pathetic in the condition of one who cherishes the ambition of being a good man, but who has not informed himself of the present "state of the art."

Now and then an ethical revolution takes place. New ideals are proclaimed, and in their light all things are judged. The public conscience becomes sensitive in regard to courses of conduct which heretofore had been unchallenged. Every such advance involves a waste in established reputations. There are always excellent men who are not aware of what has been going on. They keep on conforming scrupulously to the old stand-

ards, being good in the familiar ways that were
commended in their youth. After a time they
find themselves in an alien world, and in that
world they are no longer counted among the best
people. The tides of moral enthusiasm are all
against them. The good man feels his solid
ground of goodness slipping away from under
him. Time has played false with his moral con-
ventionalities. He is like a polar bear on a fast-
diminishing iceberg, growling at the Gulf Stream.

When a great evil has been recognized by the
world, there is a revision of all our judgments. A
new principle of classification is introduced, by
which we differentiate the goats from the sheep.
It is hard after that to revive the old admirations.
The temperance agitation of the last century has
not abolished drunkenness, but it has made the
conception of a pious, respectable drunkard seem
grotesque. It has also reduced the business of
liquor-selling to a decidedly lower place in the
esteem of the community. When we read to-day
of the horrors of the slave trade, we reconstruct in
our imagination the character of the slave trader,
— and a brutal wretch he is. But in his day the
Guinea captain held his own with the best. He

was a good husband and father, a kind neighbor,
a generous benefactor. President Ezra Stiles of
Yale College, in his "Literary Diary," describes
such a beautiful character. It was when Dr. Stiles
was yet a parish minister in Newport that one
of his parishioners died, of whom he wrote:
"God had blessed him with a good Estate and
he and his Family have been eminent for Hospi-
tality to all and Charity to the poor and afflicted.
At his death he recommended Religion to his
Children and told them that the world was nothing.
The only external blemish on his Character was
that he was a little addicted to the marvelous in
stories of what he had seen in his Voyages and
Travels. But in his Dealings he was punctual,
upright, and honest, and (except as to the Flie in
the Oynment, the disposition to tell marvelous
Stories of Dangers, Travels, &c.), in all other
Things he was of a sober and good moral character, respected and beloved of all, so as to be almost
without enemies. He was forward in all the concerns of the Church and Congregation, consulting
its Benefit and peaceably falling in with the general sense without exciting quarrels, parties, &c.,
and even when he differed from his Brethren he

so differed from them that they loved him amidst the differences. He was a peaceable man and promoted Peace."

It was in 1773 that this good man died in the odor of sanctity. It is quite incidentally that we learn that "he was for many years a Guinea captain, and had no doubt of the slave trade." His pastor suggests that he might have chosen another business than that of "buying and selling the human species." Still, in 1773, this did not constitute an offense serious enough to be termed a fly in the ointment. In 1785, Dr. Stiles speaks of the slave trade as "a most iniquitous trade in the souls of men." Much may happen in a dozen years in changing one's ideas of moral values. In another generation the civilized world was agreed that the slave trade was piracy. After that there were no fine Christian characters among the slave traders.

There is evidence that at the present time there is an awakening of the social conscience that threatens as great a revolution as that which came with the abolition of the slave trade. Business methods which have been looked upon as consistent with high moral character are being condemned as "the sum of all villainies." The condemnation is not yet universal, and there are still those who are not conscious that anything has happened. The Christian monopolist, ruthlessly crushing out his competitors and using every trick known to the trade, has no more doubts as to the rightfulness of his proceedings than had the good Newport captain in regard to the slave trade.

It is a good time to have his obituary written. His contemporaries appreciate his excellent private virtues, and have been long accustomed to look leniently on his public wrong-doing. The new generation, having agreed to call his methods robbery, may find the obituary eulogies amusing.

AN HOUR WITH OUR PREJUDICES

◆?◆

WE may compare the human mind to a city. It has its streets, its places of business and amusement, its citizens of every degree. When one person is introduced to another it is as if the warder drew back the bolts, and the gates were thrown open. If he comes well recommended he is given the freedom of the city. In the exercise of this freedom, however, the stranger should show due caution.

There is usually a new quarter. Here the streets are well lighted and policed, the crowds are cosmopolitan, and the tourist who wanders about looking at the shop windows is sure of a civil reply to his questions. There is no danger of highway robbers, though of course one may be taken in by confidence men. But if he be of an inquiring mind and a lover of the picturesque, he is not satisfied with this. After all, the new quarters are very much alike, and one tires after a while of shop windows. The visitor longs to explore the old town, with its winding ways, with its overhanging houses, and its mild suggestions of decay.

But in the mental city the lover of the picturesque must remember that he carries his life in his hands. It is not safe to say to a casual acquaintance, "Now I have a fair idea of that part of your mind which is like that of any other decently educated person. I have seen all the spick and span show places, and admired all the modern improvements. Where are your ruins? I should like to poke around a while in the more dilapidated section of your intellect."

Ah, but that is the Forbidden City. It is inhabited, not by orderly citizens, under the rule of Right Reason, but by a lawless crowd known as the Prejudices. They are of all sorts and conditions. Some are of aristocratic lineage. They come from a long line of hereditary chiefs, who, as their henchmen have deserted them, have retreated into their crumbling strongholds. Some are bold, roistering blades who will not stand a question; dangerous fellows, these, to meet in the dark! The majority, perhaps, are harmless folk, against whom the worst that can be said is that they have a knack of living without visible means of support.

A knowledge of human nature, as distinguished from a knowledge of moral philosophy, is a perception of the important part played by instinctive likes and dislikes, by perverse antipathies, by odd ends of thought, by conclusions which have got hopelessly detached from their premises — if they ever had any. The formal philosopher, judging others by himself, works on the assumption that man is naturally a reasoning animal, whereas experience teaches that the craving for the reasonable is an acquired taste.

Of course we all have reasons for our opinions, — plenty of them! But in the majority of cases they stand not as antecedents, but as consequents. There is a reversal of the rational order like that involved in Dr. Hale's pleasant conceit of the young people who adopted a grandmother. In spite of what intellectual persons say, I do not see how we can get along without prejudices. A prejudice is defined as " an opinion or decision formed without due examination of the facts or arguments which are necessary to a just and impartial determination." Now, it takes a good deal of time to make a due examination of facts and arguments, even in regard to a small matter. In the meantime our minds would be sadly unfurnished. If we are to make a fair show in the world, we must get our mental furniture when we set up housekeeping, and pay for it on the installment plan.

Instead of taking a pharisaic attitude toward our neighbor's prejudices, it is better to cultivate a wise tolerance, knowing that human intercourse is dependent on the art of making allowances. This is consistent with perfect honesty. There is always something to admire if the critic is sufficiently discriminating. When you are shown a bit of picturesque dilapidation, it is quite possible to enjoy it. Said the Hebrew sage, "I went by the field of the slothful, and by the vineyard of the man void of understanding; and, lo, it was all grown over with thorns, and nettles had covered the face thereof, and the stone wall thereof was broken down. Then I saw, and considered it well: I looked upon it, and received instruction."

His point of view was that of a moralist. Had he also been a bit of an artist, the sight of the old wall with its tangle of flowering briers would have had still further interest.

When one's intellectually slothful neighbor points with pride to portions of his untilled fields, we must not be too hard upon him. We also have patches of our own that are more picturesque than useful. Even if we ourselves are diligent husbandmen, making ceaseless war on weeds and vermin, there are times of relenting. Have you never felt a tenderness when the ploughshare of criticism turned up a prejudice of your own? You had no heart to harm the

Wee sleekit, cow'rin', tim'rous beastie.

It could not give a good account of itself. It had been so long snugly ensconced that it blinked helplessly in the garish light. Its

wee-bit housie, too, in ruin !
Its silly wa's the win's are strewin' !
And naething now to big a new ane.

You would have been very angry if any one had trampled upon it.

This is the peculiarity about a prejudice. It is very appealing to the person who holds it. A man is seldom offended by an attack on his reasoned judgments. They are supported by evidence and can shift for themselves. Not so with a prejudice. It belongs not to the universal order; it is his very own. All the chivalry of his nature is enlisted in its behalf. He is, perhaps, its only defense against the facts of an unfriendly world.

We cannot get along without making allowances for these idiosyncrasies of judgment. Conversation is impossible where each person insists on going back, all the time, to first principles, and testing everything by an absolute standard. With a person who is incapable of changing his point of view we cannot converse; we can only listen and protest. We are in the position of one who, conscious of the justice of his cause, attempts to carry on a discussion over the telephone with "Central." He only hears an inhuman buzzing sound indicating that the line is busy. There is nothing to do but to "hang up the 'phone."

When a disputed question is introduced, one may determine the true conversationalist by applying the method of Solomon. Let it be proposed to divide the subject so that each may have his own. Your eager disputant will be satisfied, your genial talker is aghast at the proposition, for he realizes that it would kill the conversation. Instead of holding his own, he awaits developments. He is in a mood which can be satisfied with something less than a final judgment. It is not necessary that his friend's opinions should be just; it is sufficient that they are characteristic. Whatever turn the talk may take, he preserves an easy temper. He is a heresy-hunter, — not of the grim kind that goes hunting with a gun; he carries only a camera. If he stirs up a strange doctrine he does not care to destroy it. When he gets a snap-shot at human nature he says, —

> Those things do best please me
> That befall preposterously.

An English gentleman relates a conversation he had with Prince Bismarck. The prince was inclined to take a pessimistic view of the English people. He thought that there was a degeneration in the race, which he attributed to the growing habit of drinking water. "Not that he believed that there was any particular virtue *per se* inherent in alcoholic drink; but he was sorry to hear that the old 'three bottle men' were dying out and leaving no successors. He had a suspicion that it meant shrinkage in those qualities of the English

which had made them what they were in the past,
and for which he had always felt a sincere admiration."

It would have been very easy to drift into
debate over this proposition. The English gentleman, however, defended his countrymen more
diplomatically. " I replied that with regard to
the water-drinking proclivities of my countrymen
there was a good deal of calumny connected with
the story. It is true that a certain section of English society has indeed taken to water as a bev-
erage. But to argue therefrom that the English
people have become addicted to water would be
to draw premature conclusions from insufficient
data. In this way I was able to calm Prince Bismarck's fears in regard to what the future might
bring forth, and our conversation reverted to
Royalty."

Each nation has its own set of preconceptions.
We must take them altogether, or not at all.
They are as compact and as natural a growth
as the concentric layers of an onion. Here is a
sentence from Max Müller's " Autobiography,"
thrown out quite incidentally. He has been telling
how strange it seemed, when first coming to Ox-

ford, to find that the students got along without
dueling. Fighting with swords seemed to him the
normal method of developing manliness, though
he adds that in the German universities " pistol
duels are generally preferred by theological students, because they cannot easily get a living if
the face is scarred all over."

This remark must be taken as one would take
a slice of the national onion. One assumption fits
into another. To an Englishman or an American
there is an incongruity that approaches the grotesque, — because our prejudices are different.
It all becomes a matter-of-fact statement when we
make the proper assumptions in regard to dueling
in general and theological duels in particular.
Assuming that it is necessary for theological students to fight duels, and that the congregations
are prejudiced against ministers whose faces have
been slashed by swords, what is left for the poor
theologues but pistols ? Their method may seem
more dangerous than that adopted by laymen, but
Max Müller explains that the danger is chiefly to
the seconds.

Individual peculiarities must be taken into
account in the same way. Prince Bismarck, in

dining with the Emperor, inquired the name of
the brand of champagne, which proved to be a
cheap German article. " The Emperor explained,
' I drink it from motives of economy, as I have a
large family; then again I drink it from patriotic
motives.' Thereupon I said to the Emperor,
' With me, your Majesty, patriotism stops short
in the region of my stomach.' "

It is evident that here was a difference not to
be arbitrated by reason. If the Emperor could
not understand the gastronomic limitations to the
Chancellor's patriotism, neither could the Chancellor enter into the Emperor's anxieties, as he
economized for the sake of his large family.

One cannot but wonder at the temerity of a
person who plunges into conversation with a
stranger without any preliminary scouting or
making sure of a line of retreat. Ordinary prudence would suggest that the first advances should
be only in the nature of a reconnoissance in force.
You may have very decided prejudices of your
own, but it is not certain that they will fraternize
with those of your new acquaintance. There is
danger of falling into an ambush. There are painful occasions when we remember the wisdom of

the Son of Sirach: "Many have fallen by the
edge of the sword, but not so many as have fallen
by the tongue." The mischief of it is that the
most kindly intent will not save us. The path of
the lover of mankind is beset by difficulties for
which he is not prepared. There are so many an-
tagonisms that are unpredictable.

When Nehemiah came to rebuild the walls of
Jerusalem he remarked grimly, " When Sanballat
the Horonite, and Tobiah the servant, the Am-
monite, heard of it, it grieved them exceedingly
that there was come a man to seek the welfare of
the children of Israel; " and the trouble was that
a large number of the children of Israel themselves
seem to have resented the interference with their
habitual misfortunes. The experience of Nehemiah is that of most reformers. One would suppose that the person who aims at the greatest
good for the greatest number would be greeted
with instant applause. The difficulty is that the
greatest good is just what the greatest number
will not tolerate. One does not need to believe
in human depravity to recognize the prejudice
which most persons have against anything which
is proposed as good for them. The most success-

ful philanthropists are those who most skillfully conceal their benevolent intent.

In Coleman's " Life of Charles Reade " there is a paragraph which gives us a glimpse of a prejudice that has resisted the efforts of the most learned men to eradicate it. An incident is there recorded that took place when Reade was a fellow in Magdalen College. " Just as I was about to terminate my term of office (I hope with credit to myself and the 'Varsity), an untoward incident occurred which embittered my relations for life with two very distinguished men. Professor Goldwin Smith and his friend John Conington, who belonged to us, had attempted to inaugurate a debating society. A handful of unmannerly young cubs, resenting the attempt to teach them political economy, ducked poor Conington under the college pump."

" Resenting the attempt to teach them political economy ! " — What is the source of that resentment ? What psychologist has fathomed the abyss of the dark prejudice which the natural man has against those who would improve his mind ? It is a feud which reaches back into hoar antiquity. Doubtless the accumulated grievances of genera-

tions of schoolboys have intensified the feud, but
no amelioration of educational methods has put
an end to it. In the most successful teacher you
may detect a nervous strain like that which the
trainer of wild beasts in the arena undergoes. His
is a perilous position, and every faculty must be
on the alert to hold the momentary ascendency.
A single false motion, and the unmannerly young
cubs would be upon their victim.

Must we not confess that this irrational resentment against our intellectual benefactors survives,
in spite of all discipline, into mature life ? We
may enlarge the area of our teachableness, but there
are certain subjects in regard to which we do not
care to be set right. The polite conventionality
according to which a person is supposed to know
his own business is an evidence of this sensitiveness. Of course the assumption is not justified by
facts. A man's own business is just the thing he
is conscious of not knowing, and he would give
anything in a quiet way to find out. Yet when
a candid friend ventures to instruct him, the old
irrational resentment flashes out. What we call
tact is the ability to find before it is too late what
it is that our friends do not desire to learn from

us. It is the art of withholding, on proper occasions, information which we are quite sure would be good for them.

The prejudice against our intellectual superiors, which leads us to take their well-meant endeavors in our behalf as of the nature of personal insults, is matched by the equally irrational repulsion which many superior people have for their inferiors. Nothing can be more illogical than the attitude of these gifted ones who use their gifts as bludgeons with which to belabor the rest of us. When we read the writings of men who have a stimulating sense of their own genius, we are struck by their nervous irritability whenever they mention " mediocrity." The greater number of the quarrels of the authors, which the elder Disraeli chronicled, arose from the fact that the authors had the habit of accusing one another of this vice. One would suppose mediocrity to be the sum of all villainies, and that the mediocre man was continually plotting in the night watches against the innocent man of genius; and yet what has the mediocre man done to deserve this detestation ? Poor fellow, he has no malice in him ! His mediocrity is only an afterthought. He has done his level best; his misfortune is that several million of his fellowmen have done as well.

The superior man, especially if his eminence be accidental, is likely to get a false notion of those who stand on the level below him. The biographer of an English dignitary says that the subject of his memoir was not really haughty, but " he was apt to be prejudiced against any one who seemed to be afraid of him." This is a not uncommon kind of prejudice ; and in nine cases out of ten it is unfounded. The great man should remember that most of those whose manners seem unduly respectful mean nothing personal.

As great Pompey passes through the streets of Rome, he may be pardoned for thinking meanly of the people. They appear to be a subservient lot, with no proper interests of their own, their happiness dependent on his passing smile, — and he knows how little that is worth. He sees them at a disadvantage. Let him leave his triumphal chariot, and, in the guise of Third Citizen, fall into friendly chat with First Citizen and Second Citizen, and his prejudices will be corrected. He will find that these worthy men have a much more independent and self-respecting point of view than he had thought possible. They are out for a holiday; they are critics of a spectacle, easily pleased, they will admit; but if no one except Pompey is to be seen to-day, why not make the most of him? Pompey or Cæsar, it matters not; "the play's the thing."

The origin of some of our prejudices must be sought in the childhood of the race. There are certain opinions which have come down from the cave-dwellers without revision. They probably at one time had reasons to justify them, though we have no idea what they were. There are others, which seem equally ancient, which originated in the forgotten experiences of our own childhood. The prehistoric age of myth and fable does not lie far behind any one of us. It is as if Gulliver had been educated in Lilliput, and, while he had grown in stature, had never quite emancipated himself from the Lilliputian point of view. The great hulking fellow is always awkwardly trying to look up at things which he has actually out-grown. He tries to make himself believe that his early world was as big as it seemed. Some-times he succeeds in his endeavors, and the result is a curious inversion of values.

Mr. Morley, in speaking of Lord Palmerston's foreign policy, says: "The Sultan's ability to speak French was one of the odd reasons why Lord Palmerston was sanguine of Turkish civilization." This association of ideas in the mind of the Prime Minister does seem odd till we remember that before Lord Palmerston was in the cabinet he was in the nursery. The fugitive impressions of early childhood reappear in many curious shapes. Who would be so hard-hearted as to exorcise these guiltless ghosts?

Sometimes, in reopening an old book over which long ago we had dreamed, we come upon the innocent source of some of our long-cherished opinions. Such discovery I made in the old Family Bible when opening at the pages inserted by the publisher between the Old Testament and the Apocrypha. On many a Sunday afternoon my stated hour of Bible reading was diversified by excursions into these uncanonical pages. There was a sense of stolen pleasure in the heap of miscellaneous secularities. It was like finding under the church roof a garret in which one might rummage at will. Here were tables of weights and measures, explanations about shekels, suggestions in regard to the probable length of a cubit, curious calculations as to the number of times the word "and" occurred in the Bible. Here, also, was a mysterious "Table of Offices and Conditions of Men."

I am sure that my scheme of admirations, my conception of the different varieties of human grandeur, has been colored by that "Table of Offices and Conditions of Men." It was my "Social Register" and Burke's "Peerage" and "Who's Who?" all in one. It was a formidable list, beginning with the patriarchs, and ending with the deacons. The dignity of the deacon I already knew, for my uncle was one, but his function was vastly exalted when I thought of him in connection with the mysterious personages who went before. There was the "Tirshatha, a governor appointed by the kings of Assyria,"— evidently a very great man. Then there were the "Nethinims, whose duty it was to draw water and to cleave wood." When I was called upon to perform similar services I ventured to think that I myself, had I lived in better days, might have been recognized as a sort of Nethinim.

Here, also, I learned the exact age of the world,

not announced arbitrarily, but with the several items all set down, so that I might have verified them for myself, had I been mathematically gifted. "The whole sum and number of years from the beginning of the world unto the present year of our Lord 1815 is 5789 years, six months, and the said odd ten days." I have no prejudice in favor of retaining that chronology as far as the thousands are concerned. Five thousand years is one way of saying it was a very long time. If the geologists prefer to convey the same idea by calling it millions, I am content; but I should hate to give up the "said odd ten days."

From the same Table of Offices and Conditions I imbibed my earliest philosophical prejudices; for there I learned the difference between the Stoics and the Epicureans.

The Stoics were described succinctly as "those who denied the liberty of the will." Just what this might mean was not clear, but it had an ugly sound. The Stoics were evidently contentious persons. On the other hand, all that was revealed concerning the Epicureans was that they "placed all happiness in pleasure." This seemed an eminently sensible idea. I could not but be favorably disposed toward people who managed to get happiness out of their pleasures.

To the excessive brevity of these definitions I doubtless owe an erroneous impression concerning that ancient, and now almost extinct people, the Samaritans. The name has had to me a suggestion of a sinister kind of scholarship, as if the Samaritans had been connected with some of the black arts. Yet I know nothing in their history to justify this impression. The source of the error was revealed when I turned again to the "Table of Offices and Conditions of Men" and read once more, "Samaritans, mongrel professors, half heathen and half Jew." How was I to know that the reference was to professors of religion, and not to professors of the arts and sciences?

As there are prejudices which begin in verbal misunderstandings, so there are those which are nourished by the accidental collocation of words. A noun is known by the adjectives it keeps. When we hear of dull conservatism, rabid radicalism, selfish culture, timid piety, smug respectability, we receive unfavorable impressions. We do not always stop to consider that all that is objectionable really inheres in the qualifying words. In a well-regulated mind, after every such verbal turn there should be a call to change partners. Let every noun take a new adjective, and every verb a new adverb.

Clever Bohemians, having heard so much of " smug respectability," take a dislike to respectability. But some of the smuggest persons are not respectable at all, — far from it! Serenely satisfied with their own irresponsibility, they look patronizingly upon the struggling world that owes them a living. I remember a visit from one of these gentry. He called to indicate his willingness to gratify my charitable impulses by accepting from me a small loan. If I did not believe the story of his frequent incarcerations I might consult the chaplain of the House of Correction. He evidently considered that he had a mission. He went about offering his hard and impenitent heart as a stone on which the philanthropists might whet their zeal. Smug respectability, forsooth!

From force of habit we speak of the " earnest " reformer, and we are apt to be intolerant of his lighter moods. Wilberforce encountered this prejudice when he enlivened one of his speeches with a little mirth. His opponent seized the opportunity to speak scornfully of the honorable gentleman's "religious facetiousness." Wilberforce replied very justly that "a religious man might sometimes be facetious, seeing that the irreligious did not always escape being dull."

An instance of the growth of a verbal prejudice is that which in certain circles resulted in the preaching against what was called "mere morality." What the preachers had in mind was true enough. They objected to *mere* morality, as one might say, "Mere life is not enough to satisfy us, we must have something to live on." They would have more than a bare morality. It should be clothed with befitting spiritual raiment. But the parson's zeal tended to outrun his discretion, and forgetting that the true object of his attack was the mereness and not the morality, he gave the impression that the Moral Man was the great enemy of the faith. At last the parishioner would turn upon his accuser. "You need not point the finger of scorn at me. What if I have done my duty to the best of my ability! You should not twit on facts. If it comes to that, you are not in a position to throw stones. If I am a moral man, you're another."

There are prejudices which are the result of excessive fluency of speech. The flood of words sweeps away all the natural distinctions of thought. All things are conceived of under two categories, — the Good and the Bad. If one ill is admitted, it is assumed that all the rest follow in its train. There are persons who cannot mention " the poor " without adding, " the weak, the wretched, the oppressed, the downtrodden, the suffering, the sick, the sinful, the erring," and so on to the end of the catalogue. This is very disconcerting to a young fellow who, while in the best of health and spirits, is conscious that he is rather poor. He would willingly admit his poverty were it not for the fear of being smothered under the wet blanket of universal commiseration.

When the category of the Good is adopted with the same undiscriminating ardor the results are equally unfortunate. We are prejudiced against certain persons whom we have never met. We have heard nothing but good of them, and we have heard altogether too much of that. Their characters have been painted in glaring virtues that swear at one another. We are sure

that we should not like such a combination of
unmitigated excellencies, for human nature abhors a paragon. And yet the too highly commended person may, in reality, not be a paragon
at all, but a very decent fellow. He would quickly
rise in our regard were it not for the eulogies
which hang like millstones around his neck.

It is no easy thing to praise another in such a
way as to leave a good impression on the mind
of the hearer. A virtue is not for all times. When
a writer is too highly commended for being labo-
rious and conscientious we are not inclined to
buy his book. His conscience doth make cowards
of us all. It may be proper to recommend a candidate for a vacant pulpit as indefatigable in his
pastoral labors; but were you to add, in the goodness of your heart, that he was equally indefatigable as a preacher, he would say, " An enemy
hath done this." For the congregation would suspect that his freedom from fatigue in the pulpit
was likely to be gained at their expense.

The prejudices which arise from verbal association are potent in preventing any impartial judgment of men whose names have become house-
hold words. The man whose name has become

the designation of a party or a theory is the help-less victim of his own reputation. Who takes the trouble to pry into the personal opinions of John Calvin? Of course they were Calvinistic. When we hear of the Malthusian doctrine about population, we picture its author as a cold-blooded, economical Herod, who would gladly have ordered a massacre of the innocents. Let no one tell us that the Reverend Richard Malthus was an amiable clergyman, who was greatly beloved by the small parish to which he minis-tered. In spite of all his church wardens might say, we would not trust our children in the hands of a man who had suggested that there might be too many people in the world. But in such cases we should remember that a man's theories do not always throw light upon his character. When a distinguished physician has a disease named after him, it is understood that the disease is the one he discovered, and not the one he died of.

When the Darwinian hypothesis startled the world, many pious imaginations conceived defi-nite pictures of the author of it. These pictures had but one thing in common, — their striking unlikeness to the quiet gentleman who had made

all this stir. By the way, Darwin was the innocent victim of two totally disconnected lines of
prejudice. After he had outlived the disfavor of
the theologians, he incurred the contempt of the
apostles of Culture ; all because of his modest
confession that he did not enjoy poetry as much
as he once did. Unfortunately, his scientific habit
of mind led him to say that he suspected that he
might be suffering from atrophy of the imaginative faculty. Instantly every literal-minded reader
and reviewer exclaimed, "How dreadful! What
a judgment on him!" Yet, when we stop to
think about it, the affliction is not so uncommon
as to call for astonishment. Many persons suffer
from it who are not addicted to science.

After all, these are harmless prejudices. They
are content with their own little spheres ; they ask
only to live and let live. There are others, however, that are militantly imperialistic. They are
ambitious to become world powers. Such are
those which grow out of differences in politics,
in religion, and in race.

Political animosities have doubtless been miti-
gated by freer social intercourse, which gives more

opportunities for meeting on neutral ground. It is only during a heated campaign that we think of all of the opposing party as rascals. There is time between elections to make the necessary exceptions. It is customary to make allowance for a certain amount of partisan bias, just as the college faculty allows a student a certain number of " cuts." It is a just recognition of human weakness.

Our British cousins go farther, and provide means for the harmless gratification of natural prejudices. There are certain questions on which persons are expected to express themselves with considerable fervor, and without troubling themselves as to the reasonableness of their contention. In a volume of published letters I was pleased to read one from a member of the aristocracy. He had been indulging in trivial personalities, when suddenly he broke off with " Now I must go to work on the Wife's Sister's Question; I intend to make a good stout protest against that rascally bill!" There is no such exercise for the moral nature as a good stout protest. We Americans take our exercise spasmodically. Instead of going about it regularly, we wait for some extraordinary occasion. We make it a point of sportsmanship to shoot our grievance on the wing, and we are nervously anxious lest it get out of range before we have time to take aim.

Not so the protesting Briton. He approves of the answer of Jonah when he was asked, "Doest thou well to be angry for the gourd?" Jonah, without any waste of words, replied, "I do well to be angry." When the Englishman feels that it is well for him to be angry, he finds constitutional means provided. Parliament furnishes a number of permanent objects for his disapproval. Whenever he feels disposed he can make a good stout protest, feeling assured that his indignation is well bestowed. He has such satisfaction as that which came to Mr. Micawber in reading his protest against the villainies of Uriah Heep: "Much afflicted but still intensely enjoying himself, Mr. Micawber folded up the letter and handed it with a bow to my aunt, as something she might like to keep."

These stout-hearted people have learned not only how to take their pleasures sadly, but, what is more to the purpose, how to take their sadnesses pleasantly. We Americans have, here, something to learn. We should get along better if we had a number of argument-proof questions like that in regard to marriage with the deceased wife's sister which could be warranted to recur at regular intervals. They could be set apart as a sort of public playground for the prejudices. It would at least keep the prejudices out of mischief.

Religious prejudice has an air of singularity. The singular thing is that there should be such a variety. If we identify religion with the wisdom that is from above, and which is " first pure, then peaceable, easy to be entreated, without partiality," it is hard to see where the prejudice comes in. Religious prejudice is a compound of religion and several decidedly earthly passions. The combination produces a peculiarly dangerous explosive. The religious element has the same part in it that the innocent glycerine has in nitro-glycerine. This latter, we are told, is " a compound produced by the action of a mixture of strong nitric and sulphuric acids on glycerine at low temperatures." It is observable that in the making of religious prejudice the religion is kept at a very low temperature, indeed.

We are at present in an era of good feeling. Not only is there an interchange of kindly offices between members of different churches, but one may detect a tendency to extend the same tolerance to the opposing party in the same church. This is a real advance, for it is always more difficult to do justice to those who differ from us slightly than to those whose divergence is fundamental. To love our friends is a work of nature, to love our enemies is a work of grace; the troublesome thing is to get on with those who are "betwixt and between." In such a case we are likely to fall between nature and grace as between two stools. Almost any one can be magnanimous in great affairs, but to be magnanimous in trifles is like trying to use a large screw-driver to turn a small screw.

In a recently published correspondence between dignitaries of the Church of England I find many encouraging symptoms. The writers exhibit a desire to do justice not only to the moral, but also to the intellectual, gifts of those who differ from them even slightly. There is, of course, enough of the old Adam remaining to make their judgments on one another interesting

reading. It is pleasant to see brethren dwelling
together in unity, — a pleasure seldom prolonged
to the point of satiety. Thus the Dean of Nor-
wich writes to the Dean of Durham in regard to
Dean Stanley. Alluding to an opinion, in a pre-
vious letter, in regard to Archbishop Tait, the
writer says : " I confess I should n't have ranked
him among the great men of the day. Of our
contemporaries I should have assigned that rank,
without hesitation, to little Stan, though I quite
think he did more mischief in our church and to
religion than most men have it in them to do.
Still I should say that little Stan was a great man
in his way." There you may see a mind that has,
with considerable difficulty, uprooted a prejudice,
though you may still perceive the place where
the prejudice used to be.

While the methods of the exact sciences have
had a discouraging effect on partisan and sectarian
prejudices, they seem, for the moment, to have
given new strength to those which are the result
of differences in race. Time was when Anti-Sem-
itism derived its power from religious rancor.
The cradle hymn which the Puritan mother sang
began sweetly, —

> Hush, my dear, lie still and slumber !
> Holy angels guard thy bed !

But after a while the mother thinks of the wickedness of the Jews : —

> Yet to read the shameful story
> How the Jews abused their King,
> How they served the Lord of Glory,
> Makes me angry while I sing.

In these days, the Anti-Semites are not so likely to be angry while they sing, as while they cast up their accounts.

The natural sciences discriminate between classes rather than between individuals. Sociology deals with groups, and not with persons. Anthropology acquaints us with the aboriginal and unmoralized man. It emphasizes the solidarity of the clan and the persistence of the cult. Experimental psychology is at present interested in the sub-conscious and instinctive life. For its purpose it treats a man as a series of nervous reactions. Human history is being rewritten as a branch of Natural History. Eliminating the part played by personal will, it exhibits an age-long warfare between nations and races.

This is all very well so long as we remember what it is that we are studying. Races, cults, and social groups exist and have their history. There is no harm in defining the salient characteristics of a race, and saying that, on the whole, one race is inferior to another. The difficulty comes when this rough average is made the dead line beyond which an individual is not allowed to pass.

In our Comedy of Errors, which is always slipping into tragedy, there are two Dromios on the stage, — the Race and the Individual. The Race is an abstraction which can bear any amount of punishment without flinching. You may say anything you please about it and not go far wrong. It is like criticising a composite photograph. There is nothing personal about it. Who is offended at the caricatures of Brother Jonathan or of John Bull? We recognize certain persistent national traits, but we also recognize the element of good-humored exaggeration. The Jew, the Slav, the Celt, the Anglo-Saxon have existed for ages. Each has admired himself, and been correspondingly disliked by others. Even the Negro as a racial abstraction is not sensitive. You may, if you will, take up the text, so much quoted a generation ago, " Cursed be Canaan; a servant of servants shall he be. . . . God shall enlarge Japheth, and he shall dwell in the tents of Shem; and Canaan shall be his servant." Dromio Africanus listens unmoved to the exegesis of Petroleum V. Nasby and his compeers at the Crossroads: " God cust Canaan, and sed he shood be a servant forever. Did he mean us to pay him wages? Not eny: for ef he hed he wood hev ordered our tastes and habits so es we shood hev hed the wherewithal to do it."

The impassive Genius of Africa answers the Anglo-Saxon: " If it pleases you to think that your prejudice against me came out of the Ark, so be it. If you find it agreeable to identify yourself with Japheth who shall providentially be enlarged, I may as well be Canaan."

So long as the doctrinaires of the Crossroads are dealing only with highly generalized conceptions no harm is done. But now another Dromio appears. He is not a race; he is a person. He has never come that way before, and he is bewildered by what he sees and hears. Immediately he is beset by those who accuse him of crimes which some one who looks like him has committed. He

is beaten because he does not know his place;
how can he know it, stumbling as he does upon
a situation for which he is altogether unprepared?
It is an awkward predicament, this of being born
into the world as a living soul. Under the most
favorable conditions it is hard for the new arrival
to find himself, and adjust himself to his environment. But this victim of mistaken identity
finds that he has been judged and condemned
already. When he innocently tries to make the
most of himself a great uproar is created. What
right has he to interfere with the preconceived
opinions of his betters? They understand him,
for have they not known him for many generations?

Poor man Dromio! Whether he have a black
skin or a yellow, and whatever be the racial type
which his features suggest, the trouble is the same.
He is sacrificed on the altar of our stupidity.
He suffers because of our mental color-blindness,
which prevents our distinguishing persons. We
see only groups, and pride ourselves on our de-
fective vision. By and by we may learn to be a
little ashamed of our crudely ambitious generalizations. A finer gift is the ability to know a man

when we see him. It may be that Nature is
"careful of the type," and "careless of the single
life." If that be so, it may be the part of wisdom
for us to give up some of our anxieties about the
type, knowing that Nature will take care of that.
Such relief from excessive cosmic responsibility
will give us much more time for our proper work,
which is to deal justly with each single life.

HOW TO KNOW THE FALLACIES

❧

MY friend Scholasticus was in a bad way. He had been educated before the elective system came in, and he had a pathetic veneration for the old curriculum. It was to him the sacred ark, now, alas, carried away into the land of the Philistines. He cherished it as a sort of creed containing the things surely to be learned by a gentleman, and whoso hath not learned these things, let him be anathema. In meeting the present-day undergraduates, it was hard to say which amazed him most, the things they knew or the things they did not know. Perhaps the new knowledge seemed to him the more uncouth.

" The intellectual world," he would say, "is topsy-turvy. What is to be expected of a generation that learns to write before it learns to read, and learns to read before it learns to spell, — or rather which never does learn to spell. Everything begins wrong end foremost. In my day small children were supposed to be 'pleased with a rattle, tickled with a straw,' until such time as they were old enough to be put to stiff work on the First Reader. Nowadays, the babes begin with the esoteric doctrine of their playthings. Even the classics of infancy are rationalized. I was about to buy a copy of 'Mother Hubbard and her Dog' for a dear young friend, when I discovered that it was a revised version. The most stirring incident was given thus, —

> She went to the baker's to buy some bread,
> And when she came back the dog looked dead.

That was n't the way the tale was told to me. I was told that the poor dog was dead, and I believed it. That did n't prevent my believing a little while after that the doggie was dancing a jig. I took it for granted that that was the way dogs did in Mother Hubbard's day. Nowadays, the critics in bib and tucker insist that the story must conform to what they have prematurely learned about the invariable laws of nature.

"I should n't mind this if they kept on reasoning. But it 's a false start. After the wide generalizations of infancy have been forgotten, the youth begins to specialize. He takes a small slice of a subject, ignoring its more obvious features and its broader outlines. He has a contempt for general ideas. What we studied, he takes for granted. He's very observing, but he does n't put two and two together. There they stand in his mind, two separate ideas, politely ignoring one another, because they have not been properly introduced. The result of all this is evident enough. How many people do you come across with whom it is a pleasure to hold an argument? Not many! They don't know the rules of the game. You can't enter a drawing-room without hearing questions discussed in a way possible only to those whose early education in the art of reasoning had been neglected. The chances are that every one of the fallacies we learned about in Whately could appear in good society without anybody being able to call them by their Latin names.

"'Does n't this follow from that?' the facile talker asks, as if that were all that is necessary to constitute a valid argument. Of course it follows; his assertions follow one another like a flock of sheep. But what short work our old Professor would have made with these plausible sequences!

"What a keen scent the old man had for fallacies! Even when the conclusion was obviously sound, he insisted that we should come by it honestly. He would never admit that in such matters the end justifies the means. I remember his merciless exposure of the means by which some unscrupulous metaphysicians accumulated their intellectual property. His feeling about the 'Undistributed Middle' was much the same as that of Henry George about the 'Unearned Increment.' How he used to get after the moonshiners who were distilling arguments by the illicit process of the major term! In these days the illicit process goes on openly. The growth of the real sciences does not in the least discourage the pseudosciences. It rather seems to stimulate them.

"For many persons, a newly discovered fact is simply a spring-board from which they dive into a bottomless sea of speculation. They pride themselves on their ability to jump at conclusions, forgetting that jumping is an exercise in which the lower orders excel their betters. If an elephant could jump as far, in proportion to his weight, as a flea, there would be no holding him on the planet. Every new discovery is followed by a dozen extravagances, engineered by the Get-wise-quick people. There is always some Young Napoleon of Philosophy who undertakes to corner the truth-market. It's like what happened at the opening of Oklahoma Territory. Before the day set by the government when they all were to start fair in their race for farms, a band of adventurers called 'Sooners' smuggled themselves across the line. When the *bona fide* settler arrived on his quarter-section, he found an impudent Sooner in possession. You can't find any fresh field of investigation that is n't claimed by these Sooners. It all comes because people are no longer educated logically."

When Scholasticus was in this mood, it was difficult to do anything with him. It was in vain to tell him that he was narrow, for, like all narrow men, he took that as a compliment. It is the broad way, he reminded me, that leads to intellectual destruction. Still, I attempted to bring him to a better frame of mind.

" Scholasticus," said I, " the old order changes. You are a survivor of another period. You were educated according to a logical order. You learned to spell out of a Spelling Book, and to

read out of a Reader, and to write not by following the dictates of your own conscience, but
by following the copy in a Copy Book; and
you learned to speak correctly by committing to
memory the rules of grammar and afterwards the
exceptions."

"And it was a good way, too," interrupted
Scholasticus. "It gave us a respect for law and
order, to learn the rules and to abide by them.
Now, I understand, they don't have grammar, but
'language work.' The idea is, I suppose, that if
the pupils practice the exceptions they need n't
bother about the rules. When I studied geography, we began with a definition of the word geography, after which we were told that the earth
is a planet, and that three fourths of its surface
is water, a fact which I have never forgotten.
Nowadays they hold that geography, like charity,
should begin at home, so the first thing is to make
a geodetic survey of the back yard. By the time
they work up to the fact that the earth is a planet,
the pupils have learned so many other things that
it makes very little impression on their minds."

"Scholasticus," said I, "I was saying the old
order changes lest one good custom should cor-

rupt the educational world. They were great people for rules in your day. It was an inheritance from the past. You remember the anecdote of Ezekiel Cheever, head master of the Boston Latin School, who taught Cotton Mather Latin. A pupil writes, 'My master found fault with the syntax of one word, which was not so used heedlessly, but designedly, and therefore I told him there was a plain grammar rule for it. He angrily replied that there was no such rule. I took the grammar and showed the rule to him. Then he said, "Thou art a brave boy. I had forgot the rule."' That takes us back to a time when there was a superstitious reverence for rules. We don't reason so rigidly from rules now, we develop the mind according to a chronological rather than a logical order. We let the ideas come according to the order of nature."

At this, the wrath of Scholasticus bubbled over. "'The order of nature'! The nature of what? A cabbage head grows according to an order natural to cabbages. But a rational intelligence is developed according to the laws of reason. The first thing is to formulate the laws, and then to obey them. Logic has to do with the laws of rational thought, just as grammar has to do with the laws of correct speech. Nowadays, the teacher seems to be afraid of laying down the law. I visited a model school the other day. It was n't a school at all, according to the definition in the old-fashioned book I used to read: 'A school is a place where children go to study books. The good children when they have learned their lessons go out to play, the idle remain and are punished.' According to the modern method, it is the teacher who must remain to be punished for the idleness of her pupils. It 's her business to make the lessons interesting. If their attention wanders, she is held responsible. The teacher must stay after hours and plan new strategic moves. She must 'by indirections find directions out,' — while the pupil is resisting one form of instruction, she suddenly teaches him something else. In this way the pupil's wits are kept on the run. No matter how they scatter, there is the teacher before him."

"Why is not that a good way?" I said. "It certainly brings results. The pupil gets on rapidly. He learns a lesson before he knows it."

"He never does know it," growled Scholasticus. "And what's worse, he does n't know that he does n't know it. By this painless method he has never been compelled to charge his mind with it and to reason it out. And besides, it 's death on the teacher. Ezekiel Cheever taught that Boston Latin School till he was over ninety years old, and never had a touch of nervous prostration. He did n't have to lie awake planning how to hold the rapt attention of his pupils. If there was any chance of the grammar rules not being learned, he let them do the worrying. It was good for them. There was a race of sturdy thinkers in those days. They knew how to deal with knotty problems. If they survived the school, they could not be downed in the town meeting."

"Scholasticus," I said, "I don't like the way you talk. The trouble with you is that you took your education too hard. I fancy that I see every lesson you ever learned sticking out of your consciousness like the piles of stones in a New Hampshire pasture. They are monuments of industry, but they lack a certain suavity. You are doing what most Americans do, — whenever they find anything wrong they lay the blame on the public schools. Just because some of the younger men

at your club argue somewhat erratically, you
blame the whole modern system of education.
It's a way you clever people have, — you are not
content with one good and sufficient reason for
your statement of fact. You must reinforce it by
another of a more general character. It makes me
feel as I do when, a faucet needing a new washer,
I send for a plumber, — and behold twain! One
would be enough, if he would attend strictly to
business. Every system has its failures. If that
of the present day seems to have more than its
share, it is because its failures are still in evidence,
while those of your generation are mostly forgotten. Oblivion is a deft housemaid, who tidies up
the chambers of the Past, by sweeping all the
dust into the dark corners. On the other hand,
you drop into the Present amid the disorder of
the spring cleaning, when everything is out on
the line. If you could recall the shining lights in
your Logic class, you might admit that some of
them had the form of reasoning without the power
thereof. It was in your day, was n't it, that the criticism was made on the undergraduate thesis : —

> Although he wrote it all by rote,
> He did not write it right.

I could n't help thinking of those lines when I was listening just now to your reasoning. The real point, Scholasticus, is this, which seems to have escaped you. You talk of the laws of the mind. When you were in college it seemed a very simple thing to formulate these laws. There was no Child Psychology, giving way before you knew it to Adolescence, where everything was quite different. There was no talk about subliminal consciousness, where you could n't tell which was consciousness and which was something else. The mind in your day came in one standard size."

"Yes," said Scholasticus, "when we were in the Academy, we had Watts on the Mind. Watts treated his subject in a straightforward way; he had nothing about nervous reactions; he gave us plain Mind. When we got into college we had Locke on the Understanding. When it was time to take account of conscience, we had Paley's 'Moral Science.' This, with the 'Evidences,' made a pretty good preparation for life."

"So it did," I said, "and you have done credit to your training. But since that time Psychologists have made a number of discoveries which render it necessary to revise the old methods."

Seeing that he, for the first time, was giving me his attention, I thought that it might be possible to win him away from that futile and acrid criticism of the present course of events, which is the besetting sin of men of his age, to the more fruitful criticism by creation.

"Scholasticus," I said, "here is your opportunity. You complain that Logic is going out. The trouble is that it has been taught in an antiquated way. The logicians followed the analogy of mathematics. They invented all sorts of formal figures and diagrams, and were painfully abstract. When you were learning to reason, you had to commit to memory a formula like this: 'Every y is x; every z is y; therefore every z is x. *E.g.*, let the major term (which is represented by x) be "One who possesses all virtue," the minor term (z) "Every man who possesses one virtue," and the middle term (y) "Every man who possesses prudence," and you have the celebrated argument of Aristotle that "the virtues are inseparable."'

"Now you can't make the youth of this generation submit to that kind of argumentation. They are willing to admit the virtues are inseparable, if you say so, but they are not going to take time to figure it out. You can't arouse their interest by demonstrating that 'If A is B, C is D C is not D, therefore A is not B.' They say, 'What of it?' They refuse to concern themselves about the fate of letters of the alphabet. Such methods prejudice them against Logic. They prefer not to reason at all, rather than do it in such an old-fashioned way. Besides, they have peeped into the Psychology for Teachers, and they know their rights. Such teaching is not good pedagogics. The youthful mind must be shielded from abstractions; if it is not, there's no knowing what might happen. It will not do to go at your subject in such a brutal way. This is the age of the concrete and the vital. Things are observed in the state of nature. The birds must be in the bush, and the fishes in the water, and the flowers must be caught in the very act of growing. That's what makes them interesting. If the youthful mind is to be induced to love Nature, Nature must do her prettiest for the youthful mind. Otherwise it will be found that the mental vacuum abhors Nature.

" If there is to be a revival of Logic, it must be attached to something in which people are already interested. People are interested in biological processes. They like to see things grow, and to help in the process as far as they can without disturbing Nature. Why don't you, Scholasticus, try your hand at a text-book which shall insinuate a sufficient knowledge of the principles of sound reasoning, under the guise of Botany or Hygiene or Physical Culture, or some of the branches that are more popular? I believe that you could make a syllogism as interesting as anything else. All you have to do is to make people think that it is something else."

At the time Scholasticus only sniffed scornfully at my suggestion; but not many days had passed before I began to notice a change in his demeanor. Instead of his usual self-sufficiency, there came into his eyes a wistful plea for appreciation. He had the chastened air of one who no longer sits in the chair of the critic, but is awaiting the moment when he shall endure criticism.

From such signs as these I inferred that Scholasticus was writing a book. There is nothing that so takes the starch out of a man's intellect and reduces him to a state of abject dependence on the judgment of his fellow beings as writing a

book. For the first question about a book is not,
" Is it good? " but, " Will anybody read it ? "
When this question is asked, the most commonplace individual assumes a new importance. He
represents the Public. The Author wonders as to
what manner of man he is. Will he like the Book ?

I was not therefore surprised when one day
Scholasticus, in a shamefaced way, handed me
the manuscript of a work entitled, " How to Know
the Fallacies; or Nature-Study in Logic."

In these pages Scholasticus shows a sincere
desire to adapt himself to a new order of things.
He no longer stands proudly on the quarter-deck
of the good ship Logic, with a sense of fathomless
depths of rationality under the keel. Logic is a
poor old stranded wreck. His work is like that
of the Swiss Family Robinson: to carry off the
necessities of life and the more portable luxuries,
and to use them in setting up housekeeping on
the new island of Nature-Study.

I cannot say that he has been entirely successful in making the art of reasoning a pleasant out-
of-door recreation. He has not altogether overcome the stiffness which is the result of his early
education. In treating thought as if it were a

vegetable, he does not always conceal the fact that it is *not* a vegetable. There are, therefore, occasional jolts as he suddenly changes from one aspect of his subject to another.

I was, however, much pleased to see that, instead of ambitiously attempting to treat of the processes of valid reasoning, he has been content to begin with those forms of argumentation which are more familiar.

His preface does what every good preface should do : it presents the Author not at his worst nor at his best, but in a salvable condition, so that the reader will say, " He is not such a bad fellow, after all, and doubtless when he gets warmed up to his work he will do better." It may be as well to quote the Preface in full.

" Careless Reader, in the intervals between those wholesome recreations which make up the more important portion of life, you may have sometimes come upon a thought. It may have been only a tiny thoughtlet. Slight as it was in itself, it was worthy of your attention, for it was a living thing. Pushing its way out of the fertile soil of your subconscious being, it had come timidly into the light of day. If it seemed to you

unusual, it was only because you have not cultivated the habit of noticing such things. They are
really very common.

"If you can spare the time, let us sit down together and pluck up the thoughtlet by the roots
and examine its structure. You may find some
pleasure, and perhaps a little profit, in these native
growths of your mind.

"When you take up a thought and pull it to
pieces, you will see that it is not so simple as it
seems. It is in reality made up of several thoughts
joined together. When you try to separate them,
you find it difficult. The connective tissue which
binds them together is called inference. When
several thoughts growing out of the same soil are
connected by inference, they form what is called
an argument. Arguments, as they are found in
the state of Nature, are of two kinds; those that
hang together, and those that only seem to hang
together; these latter are called Fallacies.

"In former times they were treated as mere
weeds and were mercilessly uprooted. In these
days we have learned to look upon them with a
kindlier eye. They have their uses, and serve to
beautify many a spot that otherwise would remain

barren. They are the wild flowers of the intellectual world. I do not intend to intrude my own
taste or to pass judgment on the different varieties; but only to show my readers how to know
the fallacies when they see them. It may be said
that mere nomenclature is of little value. So it
is in itself; yet there is a pleasure in knowing the
names of the common things we meet every day.
The search for fallacies need never take one far
afield. The collector may find almost all the
known varieties growing within his own enclo-
sure.

"Let us then go out in the sunshine into the
pleasant field of thought. There we see the arguments — valid and otherwise — as they are growing. You will notice that every argument has
three essential parts. First is the root, called by
the old logicians in their crabbed language the
Major Premise. Growing quite naturally out of
this is the stem, called the Minor Premise; and
crowning that is the flower, with its seed vessels
which contain the potentialities of future arguments, — this is called the Conclusion.

"Let the reader observe this argument: 'Every
horse is an animal;' that is the root thought.

'Sheep are not horses;' that is the stem shooting into the air. 'Therefore, sheep are not animals;' that is the conclusion, the full corn in the ear.

"There is a pleasing impression of naturalness about the way in which one thought grows out of that which immediately preceded it. There is a sudden thrill when we come to the 'therefore,' the blossoming time of the argument. We feel that we are entering into one of Nature's secret processes. Unless our senses are deceiving us, we are actually reasoning.

"After a while, when curiosity and the pride of possession lead us to look more carefully at our treasure, we are somewhat surprised. It is not as it seemed. A little observation convinces us that, in spite of our argumentation, sheep are animals, and always have been. Thus, quite by accident, and through the unaided exercise of our own faculties, we have come upon one of the most ancient forms of reasoning, one that has engaged the attention of wise men since Aristotle, — a fallacy."

In the opening chapters, Scholasticus gives a description of the more common fallacies, with an account of their habits of growth and of the soils in which they most flourish. "*Petitio Principii*, or begging the question. This is a very pretty little fallacy of vine-like habit. It is found growing beside old walls, and wherever it is not likely to be disturbed. It is easily propagated from slips, each slip being capable of indefinite multiplication, the terminal buds sending down new roots, and the process of growth going on continuously. So tenacious is it that it is practically impossible to eradicate the *petitio*, when once it has fairly established itself. It recommends itself on the ground of economy. In most arguments the attempt is made to prove one thing by means of another thing. This, of course, involves a considerable waste of good material. In begging the question, by means of one proposition we are enabled to prove a proposition that is identical with it. In this way an idea may be made to go a long way.

" The most familiar variety of this fallacy is that known as the Argument in a Circle. To those who are fond of arguments, but who can afford very little mind space for their cultivation, this is an almost ideal fallacy. It requires only the slightest soil, deriving its nutriment almost wholly from the air, and reproducing itself without the slightest variation in type.

"Its hardiness and exuberant efflorescence make it desirable for many purposes. It is useful as a screen to hide the more unsightly parts of one's intellectual grounds. Often, too, there may be an argumentative structure that has fallen into decay. Its real reason for existence is no longer obvious, yet it may have associations which make us reluctant to tear it down. In such a case, nothing is easier than to plant a slip of the circular argument. In a short time the old ruin becomes a bower, covered with an exuberant efflorescence of rationality. This argument is to be recommended for a **Woman's Hardy Garden of Fallacies.**

"It is one which gives great pleasure to a home-loving person who finds satisfaction in that which is his own. Often have I seen a householder sitting under its sweet shade, well content. He was conscious of having an argument which answered to all his needs, and which protected him alike from the contradiction of sinners and from the intrusive questioning of the more critical sort of saints. He had such satisfaction as came to Jonah, when the booth he had constructed, with such slight skill as belonged to an itinerant preacher, was covered by the luxuriant gourd vine. Things were not going as he had expected in Nineveh, and current events were discrediting his prophecies, but Jonah 'rejoiced with great joy over the gourd.'

"I may be pardoned, in treating the circular argument, for deviating, for a moment, from the field of botany into the neighboring field of zoölogy. For after all, the same principles hold good there also, and as we are forming the habit of looking at thought as a kind of plant, we may also consider it as a kind of animal, — let us say, if you please, a goldfish. You have often paused to watch the wonders of marine life as epitomized in a glass globe upon your centre-table. Those who go down to the sea in ships have doubtless seen more of the surface of waters, but they have not the same facilities for looking into its interior life that you have in your aquarium. A school of goldfishes represent for you the finny monsters of the deep. You see the whole world they move in. The encircling glass is the firmament in the midst of the waters. The goldfishes go round and round, and have a very good time, and have many adventures, but they never get out of their crystal firmament. You may leave them for half a day, but when you come back you know just where to find them. An aquarium is a much safer place for goldfishes to swim in than the ocean; to be sure, they do not get on far, but on the other hand they do not get lost, and there are no whales or even herrings, to make them afraid. There is the same advantage in doing our reasoning in a circle. We can keep up an argument much longer when we are operating in friendly waters and are always near our base of supplies. The trouble with thinking straight is, that it is likely to take us too far from home. The first we know we are facing a new issue. From this peril we are saved by the habit of going round and round. He who argues and runs away from the real difficulty lives to argue another day, and the best of it is the argument will be just the same.

" *Argumentum ad Hominem.* This is a large family, containing many interesting varieties. The *ad hominem* is of parasitic growth, a sort of logical mistletoe. It grows not out of the nature of things, but of the nature of the particular mind to which it is addressed. In the cultivation of this fallacy it is only necessary to remember that each mind has its weak point. Find out what this weak point is, and drop into it the seed of the appropriate fallacy, and the result will exceed your fondest anticipation.

"Again with the reader's kind permission, I will stray from the field of botany; this time into that of personal experience. At the risk of falling into obsolete and discredited methods of instruction, I will ask you for the moment to look in and not out.

"Dear Reader, often, when reasoning with yourself, especially about your own conduct, you have found comfort in a syllogism like this: —

I like to do right.
I do what I like.
Therefore, I do what is right.

The conclusion is so satisfactory that you have no heart to look too narrowly at the process by which it is attained. When you do what you like, it is pleasant to think that righteousness is a by-product of your activity. Moreover, there is a native generosity about you which makes you

willing to share with others the more lasting bene-
fits which may ensue. You are ready to believe
that what is profitable to you must also be profitable to them in the long run, — if not in a material, then in a spiritual way. All the advantage
that comes to you is merely temporary and personal. When you have reaped this scanty harvest, you do not begrudge to humanity in general
its plentiful gleanings. In your altruistic mood
you do not consider too carefully the particular
blessing which your action has bestowed on the
world; you are content with the thought that it
is a good diffused.

" When out of what is in the beginning only
a personal gratification there grows a cosmic law,
we have the *Argumentum ad Hominem*. There are
few greater pleasures in life than that of having all
our preferences justified by our reason. There are
some persons who are so susceptible to arguments
of this kind that they never suffer from the sensation of having done something wrong, — a sensation which I can assure you is quite disagreeable.
They might suspect they had done wrong, were it
not that as soon as they begin to reason about it
they perceive that all that happened was highly to

their credit. The more they think about it, the more pleased they are with themselves. They perceive that their action was much more disinterested than, at the time, they intended. They are like a person who tumbles into the Dead Sea. He can't go under even if he tries. It is, of course, a matter of specific gravity. When a conscience is of less specific gravity than the moral element into which it is cast, it cannot remain submerged. The fortunate owner of such a conscience watches it with satisfaction when it serenely bobs to the surface; he advertises its superlative excellence, — ' Perfectly Pure! It floats.'

" The great use of the *ad hominem* argument is like that of certain leguminous plants which enrich the soil by giving to it elements in which it had been previously lacking. After a crop of *ad hominem* arguments has grown and been turned under, we may expect a rich harvest of more commercially valuable fallacies in the next season. To thus enrich the soil is an evidence of the skill of the culturist.

"Suppose, for example, you were to attempt to implant this proposition in the unprepared mind of an acquaintance, 'All geese are swans.' The proposition is not well received. All your friend's ornithological prejudices are against it. There is no foodstuff to support your theory.

" But suppose you prepare the soil by a crop of the *ad hominem* argument. You say to your friend, after looking admiringly at his possessions, ' It seems to me that all *your* geese are swans.' He answers cordially, ' That's just what I was thinking myself.' Now you have nicely prepared the ground for further operations.

" While controversial theologians have always had a fondness for arguments in a circle, the *ad hominem* arguments have been largely cultivated by politicians. More than a generation ago Jeremy Bentham published a work called ' Political Fallacies.' He described those that are indigenous to the British Isles. Almost all on his list were of the *ad hominem* variety. He described particularly those which could be grown to advantage in the Houses of Parliament. Since Bentham's day, much has been done in America in the way of propagating new varieties. Many of these, though widely advertised, have not yet been scientifically described. I have thought that if my present book is well received, I might publish another covering this ground. It will probably be entitled, 'Reasoning for Profit; or Success with Small Fallacies.'

"The great essential in arguments of this kind is to have a thorough knowledge of the soil. Given the right soil, and the most feeble argument will flourish. Take, for example, the arguments for the divine right of kings to rule, once much esteemed by court preachers. Of course the first necessity was to catch your kings. The arguments in themselves were singularly feeble, but they flourished mightily in the hotbeds of royalty. The trouble was that they did not bear transplanting.

"Half a century ago there were a dozen thrifty arguments for human slavery. They are, abstractly speaking, as good now as they ever were, but they have altogether passed out of cultivation.

"In landscape gardening groups of the *ad hominem* arguments skillfully arranged are always charming. Much discrimination is needed for the adornment of any particular spot. Suppose you were called upon to furnish fallacies for an Amalgamated Society of Esoteric Astrologers. You might safely, in such fertile soil and tropical climate, plant the most luxuriant exotics. Such airy growths, however, would be obviously inappropriate for a commercial club composed of solid business men. You would for them choose rather a sturdy perennial, for example, the *argumentum ad Pennsylvaniam*, or tariff-bearing argument.

"It grows thus : —

The tariff is that which conduces to our prosperity.
A tax does not conduce to our prosperity.
Therefore, a tariff is not a tax.

"Persons who have confined their logical exercises to the task of convincing impartial minds have no idea of the exhilaration which comes when one has only to convince a person of the wisdom of a course of action he has already taken. There is really no comparison between the two. There is all the difference that there is between climbing an icy hill and sliding down the same hill on a toboggan. There is no intellectual sport equal to that of tobogganing from a lofty moral premise to a congenial practical conclusion. We go so fast that we hardly know how we got to the bottom, but there we are, safe and sound. We have only to choose our company and hold on; gravitation does the rest. It is astonishing what conclusions we can come to when we do our reasoning in this pleasantly gregarious fashion.

"*Ignoratio Elenchi*, or the fallacy of irrelevant conclusion. This is not a natural species, but the result of artifice. It is a familiar kind of argument. It begins well, and it ends well, but you have a feeling that something has happened to it in the middle. You have noticed in the orchard an apple tree that starts out to be a Pippin, but when the time comes for it to bear fruit it has apparently changed its mind, and has concluded to be a Rhode Island Greening. Of course you are aware that it has not really changed its mind, for the laws of Nature are quite invariable. The whimsicality of its conduct is to be laid not upon Nature, but upon Art. The gardener has skillfully grafted one stock upon another. The same thing can be done with an argument. You have often observed the way in which a person will start out to prove one proposition and after a little while end up with the triumphant demonstration of something that is quite different. He shows such an ability at ratiocination that you cannot help admiring his reasoning powers, though it is hard to follow him. Your bewilderment comes from the fact that you had expected the original seedling to bring forth after its kind, and had not noticed the point where the scion of a new proposition had been grafted on.

" Many persons are not troubled at all when the conclusions are irrelevant. They rather like them that way. If an argument will not prove one thing, then let it prove another. It is all in the day's work. To persons with this tolerant taste the variety afforded by the use of the *ignoratio elenchi* is very pleasing."

A chapter is given to the Cross-fertilization of Fallacies. The author shows how two half-truths brought together from two widely separated fields of thought will produce a new and magnificently variegated form of opinion. The hybrid will surpass specimens of either of the parent stocks both in size and showiness. Thus a half-truth of popular religion cross-fertilized by a half-truth of popular science will produce a hybrid which astonishes both the religious and the scientific world. If we were following the analogy of mathematics we might assume that two half-truths would make a whole truth. But when we are dealing with the marvelous reproductive powers of nature we find that they make much more than that.

Scholasticus gives a page or two to the Dwarfing of Arguments. " The complaint is sometimes heard that an argument which is otherwise satisfactory proves too much. This may seem a good fault to those whose chief difficulty is in making their arguments prove anything at all. But I assure you that it is really very troublesome to find that you have proved more than you intended. You may have no facilities for dealing with the surplus conclusions, and you may find all your plans disarranged. For this reason many persons, instead of cultivating arguments of the standard sizes which take a good deal of room, prefer the dwarf varieties. These are very convenient where one does not wish one principle to crowd out another that may be opposed to it. Persons inclined to moderation prefer to cultivate a number of good ideas without crowding. The dwarf varieties are pleasing to the cultivated taste, as they are generally exceedingly symmetrical, while full-grown ideas, especially in exposed places, are apt to impress one as being scraggly.

" Dean Swift, who had no taste for miniature

excellencies, spoke scornfully of those who plant oaks in flower-pots. I have, however, frequently seen very pleasing oaks grown in this way, and they were not in very big flower-pots, either.

" In moral reasoning, it is especially difficult to keep our conclusions moderate enough for our convenience. An ordinary argument always tends to prove too much. This is disconcerting to those who are endeavoring to live up to their favorite text, ' Be not overmuch righteous.' The danger of overmuchness is obviated by cultivating the fashionable dwarf varieties of righteousness.

"Various methods of dwarfing are practiced with success. Training will do much; you have seen trees dwarfed by tying them to a trellis or against a wall or to stakes, and preventing their growth beyond the prescribed limits. Incessant pruning is necessary, and each new growth must be vigorously headed back. By using the same means we may cultivate a number of fine ideas, and at the same time keep them fairly small."

The least satisfactory chapter is that on Pests. " It is easy enough," says Scholasticus, "to describe a pest, but it is another matter to get rid of it. The most painstaking fallacy culturist must expect to awake some morning and behold his choicest arguments laid low by some new kind of critic. There seems to be no limit to the pestiferous activity of these creatures. They are of two kinds: those that bite, cutting off the roots of the argument, and those that suck out the juices. These latter destroy the vital tissue of inference on which everything depends. I never met any one who cultivated arguments on a large scale who did not have his tale of woe.

"I had at one time a theological friend who had great reputation as a dogmatist. He had for many years a garden of fallacies which was one of the show places. It was in a sheltered situation, so that many fine old dogmas flourished which we do not often, in these days, see growing out of doors. Everything went well until the locality became infested with destructive criticism. He tried all the usual remedies without success. At last he became utterly discouraged, and cut out all the dead wood, and uprooted all the dogmas that were attacked by the pest. Since then he has given up his more ambitious plans, and he has only a simple little place where he cultivates those fruits of the spirit which are not affected by destructive criticism. It is only fair to say that he is making a very pleasant place of it.

"For the encouragement of those who are not ready to take such heroic methods, it may be said that eternal vigilance, though not a panacea, will do much. Some of the most dreaded species of critics are not so dangerous as they seem. Many persons fear the *Criticus Academicus*. I have, however, seen fallacies which survived the attacks of this species and fell easy victims to the more troublesome *Criticus Vulgaris*, or Common Gumption.

"The worst pest is what is known as the *Reductio ad Absurdum*. This is a kind of scale which grows upon a promising argument and eats out its life. It is so innocent in its appearance that at first one does not suspect its deadly character. In fact, it is sometimes taken as an agreeable ornament. After a little while the argument is covered over with a sort of dry humor. There is then no remedy."

In the chapter on the use of artificial fertilizers, Scholasticus deals particularly with statistics. He refers incidentally to their use in the cultivation of valid arguments. Their importance here is universally acknowledged. "It should be remembered," he says, "that in this case success depends upon the extreme care with which they are used. An unusual amount of discrimination is demanded in their application. For this reason, if solid conclusions, that head well, are expected, only experts of good character can be trusted to do the work.

"There is no such difficulty in the use of statistics, if the grower is content with arguments of the fallacious order. Statistics are recommended for a mulch. By covering a bed of fallacies with a heavy mulch of miscellaneous statistical matter it is protected from the early frosts and the later drought. The ground of the argument is kept thus in a good condition. No particular care is here needed in the application of statistics; any man who can handle a pitchfork can do all that is required. I have seen astonishing results obtained in this way. No one need be deterred by the consideration of expense. In these days statistics are so cheap that they are within the reach of all. If you do not care to use the material freely distributed by the government, you can easily collect a sufficient amount for yourself.

"The best way is to prepare circulars containing

half a dozen irrelevant questions, which you send to several thousand persons, — the more the better. If you enclose stamps, those who are good-natured and conscientious will send you such odd bits of opinion as they have no other use for, and are willing to contribute to the cause of science. When the contributions are received, assort them, putting those that strike you as more or less alike in long, straight rows. Another way, which is more fancy, is that of arranging them in curves. This is called 'tabulating the results.' When the results have been thoroughly tabulated, use in the manner I have described for the protection of your favorite arguments."

In this way the book ran on for some three hundred pages. After I had read it, I congratulated Scholasticus on his effort. "You have almost succeeded," I said, "in making Logic interesting; that is, if it is Logic. Now that you have made such a good beginning, I wish you might go further. You have taught us, by a natural method, how to reason fallaciously. I wish you would now teach us how to reason correctly."

"I wish I could," said Scholasticus.

THE DIFFICULTIES OF THE PEACE-
MAKERS

TO one who aspires to "sit and shake in Rabe-
lais' easy-chair," the greeting "Peace on
Earth" is a godsend. Was ever such a provoca-
tive to satire? Did ever human nature appear in
a disguise more ridiculously transparent than when
assuming the part of Peacemaker in the midwin-
ter pantomimes, and impudently laying claim to
the very choicest beatitude? The bold masquer-
ader has not even the grace to hide his big stick,
but waves it as a wand. We are asked to believe
that the vigorous flourishes of this same big stick
prepare for the age of peace "by prophets long
foretold."

"Have you ever been to a Peace Conven-
tion?" asks the amateur cynic. "It is good fun
if you are fortunate enough to be able to watch
the proceedings from the seat of the scornful.
First come the advocates of Peace pure and sim-

ple, enthusiasts for non-resistance. As you listen
to the reports of the delegates you feel that the
time has already come when 'the lion shall eat
straw like the ox.' Your sympathies go out to
the poor beast in his sudden change of diet, —
for we of the Carnivora have no great appetite
for straw. After a time the lions are led out to
speak for themselves. Representatives of the different nations give greetings. It appears from
their remarks that the cause is one that has always been nearest to their valiant hearts. No
need to take measures to convert them, — they
have always been on the right side. What were
teeth and claws invented for, if not to enforce
peace on earth?

"Each nation points with pride to its achieve-
ments. Has not Great Britain made peace in
South Africa, and the United States of America
established it in the Philippines; and was not
Russia a while ago endeavoring to establish it in
Manchuria? Even the little powers are at work
for the same end. Is not disinterested Belgium
making peace on the banks of the Congo, with
rubber and ivory as a by-product? Has not
Holland for these many years been industriously

weeding out the malcontents in Java? The
Christian message of good will has now reached
the most remote recesses of the earth. Even the
monks in Thibet have heard the good news.
They must pay a good round sum for it, to be
sure; but what else could they expect when the
message must be carried to them away up on
the roof of the world, quite beyond the limits of
the free delivery? It's their own fault that they
never got into full connection with Christendom
before. These unsocial creatures have for generations been enjoying a selfish peacefulness of their
own. They have been like a householder who
has a telephone, but will not allow his number
to go on the book. He likes to bother other people, but will not allow them to bother him. It
has long been known that the Mahatmas in Llassa
were in the habit of projecting thought vibrations
to the ends of the earth, and muddling the brains
of the initiated; but the general public could not
reciprocate. The British expedition has changed
all that. Now when Christendom rings them up
they 've got to answer."

That word " Christendom " has a singular effect
upon the cynic. It draws out all his acrid humor;

for it seems to him the quintessence of hypocrisy.

"Christian nations! Christian civilization! A
fine partnership this, between the brutal and the
spiritual! In the pre-Christian era war was a very
simple thing. Read the record of an Israelitish
expedition in the Book of Chronicles. 'And they
went to the entrance of Gedor, even unto the
east side of the valley, to seek pasture for their
flocks. And they found fat pasture and good,
and the land was wide and quiet and peaceable;
for they of Ham had dwelt there of old. And
these written by name came in the days of Heze-
kiah, king of Judah, and smote their tents and
the habitations that were found there, and destroyed them utterly unto this day, and dwelt in
their rooms; because there was pasture there for
their flocks.'

"What an unsophisticated account of an ordinary transaction! Even the sons of Ham could
understand the motive. There was no profession
of benevolent intent, not even an eloquent reference to manifest destiny; the fat pastures were
a sufficient reason. In these days the unwilling
beneficiaries of civilization have a harder time

of it. No sooner are they dispossessed of their
lands than they are called together to rejoice over
the good work that has been done for them.
This is A. D. and not B. C. The new era began
with an angel chorus; let us all join in the re-
frain. First of all, decorum requires that the bare
facts be decently arrayed in spiritual garments.
With the skill that is the result of long practice
the ugliest fact is fitted. It is a triumph of dress-
making. The materials may be a trifle thread-
bare, but with a little fullness here and a breadth
taken out there, each garment is made as good as
new. Not a blood-stain shows."

This is a free country, and the cynic must be
allowed his fling. But if he has license to speak
his mind in regard to the simple-hearted people
who believe in Peace, we must be privileged to
say what we think of him. The truth is that we
think him to be a rather shallow-pated fellow
who has been educated above his deserts. For
all his knowing ways he has had but little knowledge of the world. He has seen the things which
are obvious, the things that are shown to every
outsider. He prides himself on his familiarity

with accomplished facts, not realizing that these belong to the world that is passing away. The interesting things to see are those which belong to the world that is in process of becoming. These are not visible from the seat of the scornful.

The sweeping accusation of hypocrisy against men or nations whenever an incongruity is perceived between a professed purpose and an actual achievement is an indication of too great simplicity of mind. It is the simplicity that is characteristic of one without experience in the work of creation.

The cynic, perceiving the shortcomings of those who " profess and call themselves Christians," greets their professions with a bitter laugh. He cannot tolerate their pretensions, and he urges them to return to a frank profession of the paganism which their deeds proclaim. Now it is eminently desirable that all who profess and call themselves Christians should *be* Christians, — but that takes time. The profession is the first step; that puts a whip into the hand of conscience. Not only do a man's friends, but particularly his enemies, insist that he shall live up to his name. It is a wholesome discipline. In a new country two or three houses set down in a howling wilderness are denominated a city. It is a mere name at first, but if all goes well other metropolitan features are added in due time. I remember a most interesting visit which I once made to a university in a new commonwealth. The university consisted of a board of regents, an unfenced bit of prairie for a "campus," a president (who was also professor of the Arts and Sciences), a janitor, and two unfinished buildings. A number of the village children took courses which, if persisted in for a number of years, might lead to what is usually termed the Higher Education. One student from out of town dwelt in solitary state in the dormitory. The president met me with great cordiality, and after showing me "the plant" introduced me to the student. It was evident that they were on terms of great intimacy, and that discipline in the university was an easy matter, owing to the fact that the student body was homogeneous.

Now it would be easy for one under such circumstances to laugh at what seemed mere pretentiousness. "It was nothing more than a small school; why not call it that and be done with it?" The reason for not doing so was that it aimed at being a university. Its name was a declaration of purpose. "Despise not the day of small things." The small things may be very real things; and then they have a trick of growing big before you know it.

In the world of creative activity the thought precedes the deed, the profession comes before the achievement. The child makes believe that he is a man, and his play is prophetic. Let us grant that multitudes who profess and call themselves Christians are only playing at Christianity; they have not yet begun to take the beatitudes seriously. It is a good thing to play at, and the play is all the time deepening into earnest work.

When it becomes earnest, it is still far from perfect; but imperfection of workmanship is no evidence of insincerity. He would be a poor critic who at the spring exhibition should accuse the artist of attempt to deceive because of his failure to achieve his professed purpose.

"Do you call that a picture of the Madonna? False-hearted hypocrite! Are you wicked enough to attempt to poison our minds and prejudice us against one who has been an object of worship?

You are foisting upon us an image of absolute imbecility."

And yet the poor artist is no hypocrite, — he is only a poor artist, that is all. He has striven to express what he has actually felt, and he has had bad luck. He has been thrilled by an image of perfect womanhood, and he sought to reproduce it for the joy of others. He wrought with sad sincerity, and this is what came of it!

In the work of creating a condition of peace and good will among men the Christian nations have not gone very far. But why twit on facts? Let us be reasonable. Why should we take it as a grievance that our birth has not been delayed till the Millennium, but that we have been placed among those who are responsible for bringing it in? There is a satisfaction in being allowed a part in the preliminary work. And what if many well-meant endeavors have come to nought? Let us not spend our time crying over the spilt milk of human kindness. It is natural that the first attempts at peacemaking should be awkward. It takes time to get the knack of it. It is foolish to reserve all our praise for perfection. That gives an unpleasant impression, such as that which we receive from a person who, when there is a call for small change, produces a bank bill of a large denomination, which he knows no one can break for him.

"Peace on earth" is not a statement of accomplished fact, but a prophecy. Now it is nothing against a prophecy that it has not yet been fulfilled. The farther off it is, the more credit to the eyes that see and to the stout hearts that patiently wait and work for it. The practical question is not "Has it come?" but "Is it on the way?" We are considering a bit of the unfinished business of the world.

First we must listen to the report of the progress already made. It is such a modest report that we must prepare our minds in order to appreciate it. The simple-minded cynic must be instructed in regard to the extreme difficulty and complexity of the work that has been undertaken. It is nothing less than the transformation of a carnivorous, not to say cannibalistic, species into an orderly society in which each member shall joyously and effectively work for the welfare of all. The first thing, of course, is to catch your cannibals. This of itself is no easy task, and has taken many centuries. It has involved a vast amount of wood-chopping and road-making, and draining of swamps and exploring of caves and dens. It is a task that is still far from accomplished. Savagery is a condition which cannot be abolished till there is a conquest of the earth itself. When the cannibals have been caught and tamed there comes the problem of keeping them alive. They must eat *something* — a point which many of the missionaries of civilization have not sufficiently considered. Ethical progress is delayed by all sorts of economic complications. When the natural man is confronted with the necessity of getting a living, robbery is the first method which suggests itself to him. When this is prohibited he turns upon his moral adviser with, " What more feasible way do you propose? " The moral adviser has then to turn from the plain path of pure ethics, and cudgel his poor wits trying to " invent a little something ingenious " to keep his pupil from starving. The clever railer at human kind who has always had a bank account to fall back upon has no idea how much time and thought have been taken up in such contrivances.

Then it should be remembered that the missionaries of civilization have not themselves been above reproach. The "multitudes of the heavenly hosts" might be heard for a moment singing of good will among men, but they did not remain to do the work. The men of good will who were to work out the plan were very human indeed. Milton, in the Hymn "On the Morning of Christ's Nativity," warns us of the long interval between the Christmas prophecy and its historical fulfillment.

> For, if such holy song
> Enwrap our fancy long,
>   Time will run back and fetch the age of gold;
> And speckled vanity
> Will sicken soon and die,
>   And leprous sin will melt from earthly mould;
>   .   .   .   .
> Yea, Truth and Justice then
> Will down return to men,
>   Orbed in a rainbow; and, like glories wearing,
> Mercy will sit between,
> Throned in celestial sheen,
>   With radiant feet the tissued clouds down steering:
> And Heaven, as at some festival,
> Will open wide the gates of her high palace hall.

But all the imagery of the gala day of peace fades away before the immediate reality.

But wisest Fate says no,
This must not yet be so.

This veto of "wisest Fate" is not absolute. It only calls a halt upon our imagination until the rest of our nature catches up with it. Mankind is not to have peace till it has suffered for it and worked for it. The workmen must do their work over and over again till they have learned the right way.

That the "Christian nations" are not hypocrites, but novices who have been making some progress toward the Christian ideal, becomes evident when we look back over their history. They are not the descendants of the simple shepherds of the plains of Bethlehem. Far from it! When they first began to "profess and call themselves Christians," they were not thinking of the beatitudes. They had not got that far.

Turn to the Heimskringla and read how King Olaf converted the pagan bonders.

"So King Olaf went into the God-house and a certain few of his men with him, and a certain few of the bonders. But when the king came whereas the gods were, there sat Thor the most honored of all the gods, adorned with gold and

silver. Then King Olaf hove up the gold-wrought
rod that he had in his hand and smote Thor that
he fell down from the stall; and therewith ran forth
all the king's men and tumbled down all the gods
from their stalls. But whiles the king was in the
God-house was Iron-Skeggi slain without, even at
the very door, and that deed did the king's men.
So when the king was come back to his folk he
bade the bonders take one of two things, either all
be christened, or else abide the brunt of battle with
him. But after the death of Skeggi there was no
leader among the folk of the bonders to raise up
a banner against King Olaf. So the choice was
taken of them to go to the king and obey his bid-
ding. Then King Olaf christened all folk that
were there and took hostages of the bonders that
they would hold to their christening. Thereafter
King Olaf caused men of his wend over all parts
of Thrandheim; and now spoke no man against
the faith of Christ. And so were all folk christened
in the country-side."

That is the way the nations of the north were
first christianized. What is the difference between
Thor and the Christ? the simple-hearted people
would ask. "The difference," said King Olaf, "is

very fundamental, and it requires little theological training to see it. It is this: the Christ is stronger. If you don't believe it, I 'll " — but they did believe it.

It is evident that there were some points in Christianity that King Olaf did not appreciate. To cultivate these fruits of the spirit required men of a different temper. Their work is not all done yet. It is progressing.

There is one complication in the work of peacemaking which has not been sufficiently considered. It is the recurrence of Youth. I have listened to the arguments against war at a great Peace Congress. The reasoning was strong, the statement of facts conclusive. War was shown to be cruel and foolish, and incredibly expensive. The audience, consisting of right-minded and very intelligent people, was convinced of the justice of the cause of Peace. Why, then, does not the cause triumph?

In such cases I am in the habit of looking about with the intent to fix the responsibility where it belongs, on those who were not at the meeting. Mature life was well represented, but there was a suspicious absence of young men in the twenties. Ah! I said, there is the difficulty. We can't be sure of lasting peace until we make it more interesting to these young absentees. They'll all be peace men by and by, but meanwhile there is no knowing what trouble they may get us into.

John Fiske traced the influence which the prolongation of infancy has had on the progress of civilization. I am inclined to think that equally great results would flow from any discovery by which the period of middle age could be prolonged beyond its present term. War would be abolished without any more ado. A uniformly middle-aged community would be immune from any attack of militant fever.

It happens, however, that every once in a while the hot passions of youth carry all before them. The account of what happened at the beginning of the civil wars in Israel is typical. King Rehoboam called a meeting of the elder statesmen of his kingdom. They outlined a policy that was eminently conciliatory. But we are told, " He forsook the counsel of the old men which they had given him, and consulted with the young men that were grown up with him and which stood by him."

That's the difficulty! The hardest thing about a good policy is to get it accepted by the people who have the power. What avails the wisdom of the old men when all the young men are "spoiling for a fight?" Something more is needed than statesman-like plans for strengthening the framework of civilization. You may have a fireproof structure, but you are not safe so long as it is crammed with highly inflammable material.

There is a periodicity in the passion for war. It marks the coming into power of a new generation. A quarter of a century from now "the good gray poet" Rudyard Kipling may be singing sweet lyrics of peace. All things come in time. The Kipling we know simply utters the sentiments of "the young men brought up with him." What he has been to his contemporaries Tennyson was to the generation before. Kipling never wrote a more scornful arraignment of peace or a more passionate glorification of war than Tennyson's "Maud."

We are listening to the invective of a youth whose aspirations have been crushed and ideals shattered by a civilization that seems to him to be soulless. He has seen something which to him is

infinitely more cruel than the battle between con-
tending hosts

Why do they prate of the blessings of peace ? we have made them
   a curse,
Pickpockets, each hand lusting for all that is not its own ;
And lust of gain, in the spirit of Cain, is it better or worse
Than the heart of the citizen hissing in war on his own hearth-
   stone ?

We are made to see the inglorious peace in
which men seek only their own ease.

Peace sitting under her olive, and slurring the days gone by,
When the poor are hovell'd and hustled together, each sex, like
   swine,
When only the ledger lives, and when only not all men lie.

From the evils of a soulless commercialism,
and from the inanities of fashion, what is the way
of escape? From the evils of peace he turns
to the heroism of war.

> I wish I could hear again
> The chivalrous battle song.
>
> .   .   .   .
>
> Ah God, for a man with heart, head, hand,
> Like some of the simple great ones gone
> For ever and ever by,
> One still strong man in a blatant land.

At last, breaking in upon the deadly stupidity

and selfishness of the common life, is the noise of
battle : —

> it lightened my despair
> When I thought that a war would arise in defence of the right,
> That an iron tyranny now should bend or cease,
> The glory of manhood stand on his ancient height,
> Nor Britain's one sole God be the millionaire.

> . . . .

> Let it go or stay, so I wake to the higher aims
> Of a land that has lost for a little her lust of gold,
> And love of a peace that was full of wrongs and shames,
> Horrible, hateful, monstrous, not to be told ;
> And hail once more to the banner of battle unroll'd !

That was an appeal to Young England, the
England that was too young to remember the
Napoleonic wars and was thirsting for an experi-
ence of its own.

We may see in such an outburst of the
militant spirit only the recrudescence of savagery.
It is better to treat it seriously, for it is something which each generation must reckon with.
Tennyson sums up the matter from the stand-
point of ardent youth : —

> Let it flame or fade, and the war roll down like a wind,
> We have proved we have hearts in a cause, we are noble still,
> And myself have awaked, as it seems, to the better mind.
> It is better to fight for the good than to rail at the ill ;
> I have felt with my native land, I am one with my kind,
> I embrace the purpose of God, and the doom assign'd.

It is easy enough to dismiss all this as mere vaporing. But it is a protest which must be heeded, for it expresses a real experience. There are things worse than war. A sordid slothfulness is worse. A cowardly acquiescence in injustice is worse. It is a real revelation when to the heart of youth comes a sudden sense of the meaning of life. It is not a treasure to be preserved with miserly carefulness. It is to be nobly hazarded. It *is* better to fight for the good than to rail, however eloquently, against the ill. To feel for one's native land, to unite in generous comradeship with one's kind, to endure hardness for a noble cause, — these things are of the essence of manhood.

In times of national peril such awakening has come. Many a man has then for the first time discovered that he has a soul. He has cried out, "Mine eyes have seen the glory of the coming of the Lord."

Now just here we peace men may see our most inspiring bit of unfinished business. War has been idealized; it is left to us to idealize peace. It cannot be done till we bring out all its heroic possibilities. If it means dull stagnation, selfish ease, the prosperity that can be measured in dollars and cents, there is sure to come a revulsion against it. The gospel of the full dinner-pail and the plethoric pocket-book does not satisfy. If the choice is between commercialism and militarism we need not wonder if many an idealist chooses the latter as the less perilous course. It seems less threatening toward the things for which he cares.

The call is for a new chivalry. Our duty is not only to keep the peace, but to make a peace that is worth keeping. This is no easy task. It means the humanizing of all our activities. Everywhere a human ideal must be placed above every other kind of success. Religion must be lifted above ecclesiasticism; and business honor above the vulgar standards of commercialism. The machinery of civilization must be made subservient to man. More careers must be opened for men of the soldierly spirit whose ambition is for service. The new generation must be shown what opportunities the world's business and politics offer to greathearted gentlemen who are willing to risk something for a cause. The kind of peace which the world needs cannot be had for the asking. It comes high, — but it is worth the price.

THE LAND OF THE LARGE AND CHARITABLE AIR

❦

*Are you not constrayned (my fellow Academicks) to sub-
scribe to this my opinion that the knowledge of no nation is so
necessary as the searching out of a man's own Country and the
manners thereof and the right understanding of that Common-
weale whereof each one of us is a part and member. The Lamiæ
that are a certaine kind of monsters are laughed at in the Poeti-
call Fables in that they were so blinde at home that they could
not see their own affaires, could foresee nothing; but when they
were once gone from home they were accounted the most sharpe-
sighted and curious searchers of all others. . . . [Are not they]
very ridiculous when as by taking long voyages unto farre remote
people, after they have curiously sought out all matters amongst
them are ignorant of the principall things at home and know not
what is contayned within the precincts of their country, and are
reckoned altogether strangers on their native soile?*— Coryat's
Crudities.

THE remark that Boston is not so much a
place as a state of mind is one of the highest
compliments ever paid to that city. Places are
common enough, the maps are dotted with them,
but a state of mind is a mark of distinction. The
Bostonian enjoys his state of mind none the less

because he is aware that outsiders are not always able to enter into it.

Only those places which have become symbolic of mental or moral traits are remembered. Sodom and Gomorrah were once towns of some commercial importance. We think of them, however, not as trade centres, but as sins. Babylon, according to a doctrine of spiritual correspondences long since established, is another name for proud and cruel worldliness. It is likely so to remain, in spite of the discovery of clay tablets which show that many of its people were estimable citizens who practiced domestic economy and collected their debts by due process of law. All we have to say is that those who acted in this commonplace way were not typical, — in fact, they were quite un-Babylonian. In like manner, Zion represents no longer a hill whose altitude may be prosaically estimated according to the metric system. It is a highly exalted frame of pious joy.

It is strange that, with all the ingenuity that has been shown in inventing new text-books for the use of schools, no one has compiled a Psychological Geography. The materials are ample. It only needs some one with a scientific imagination, or, rather, with a capacity for writing imaginative science, to make it a success. Eliminating those communities whose states of mind are so mixed as to be unclassifiable, the way would be clear for a very pretty series of generalizations. There would be maps with isothermal lines uniting places of equal degrees of warmth of temperament or frigidity of manner. Weather charts would show the direction of the various winds of doctrine and the storm centres, religious and political. The theory of moral cyclones and anti-cyclones would be adequately explained. There would be maps in colors indicating the communities situated on the plateaus of conscious ethical and intellectual superiority. These often rise into the arid, or at least semi-arid, belt. In sharp contrast with these are the luxuriant bottom lands, where less favored peoples dwell in happy ignorance of their low estate. The "principal products" would be graphically illustrated. One section, being without natural resources, is given over to the manufacture of novelties, while another is rich in fossils. The distribution of fads may be shown to advantage. Some localities are almost barren, while others are naturally faddy.

When he comes to the Points of the Compass the most matter-of-fact psychological geographer will forget the cold mannerisms of his science and become poetical. North, South, East, West, these are vast symbols of psychic forces. He would not think of putting at the head of the chapter the picture, from the old Geography, of the disconsolate urchin with his face to the north and his arms extended in rigid but reluctant testimony to the fact that " East is East and West is West." What does this featureless boy know of those tremendous forces whose age-long contests have made the history of the world ? What does he know of the hardiness and the prowess that make the true North ? If he were forcibly turned around, his face would be as expressionless as ever. Such a mannikin never felt a sudden longing for " a beaker full of the warm South."

Art must be called to the aid of science. Each point of the compass has an expression of its own. One should be able by looking at the face of the man in the picture to know the direction. There is no mistaking the qualities which grow only where there is a northerly exposure. The Orient and the Occident are not to be confounded.

Were some affluent citizen to endow a chair of psycho-geographical science in one of our leading universities, especial attention should be paid to the teaching of Systematic Americanism. It is a branch now much neglected. The professor should take pains to instruct his "fellow Academicks" in the manners and customs of their own country, so that they should no longer be reckoned strangers on their native soil. They should be taught to avoid entangling analogies drawn from the experience of other lands, and to look directly at the subject-matter. When they see something going wrong, they should not jump at the conclusion that it is a repetition of the classic tragedy of the Decline and Fall of the Roman Empire, — for it may be something quite different. When there is a popular movement on the prairies, they should not begin to talk of the French Revolution and of the excesses of the proletariat. Before they talk in European fashion of the "classes and the masses," they should make certain that we have such things, and if we have, that there is a sure way of telling which is which. The Old-World generalizations about the upper and lower and middle classes should be well shaken before using.

Those who elect the course in Americanism should be taught to overcome the nervous fright to which bookish people are subject at the appearance of any man in public life who shows signs of unusual virility. It is a weakness of those who are more familiar with the careers of Cæsar and Napoleon than with the temper of their fellow-citizens. In the early seventies there were academic minds thoroughly convinced that they were watching the Republic in its death struggle with Cæsarism. Curiously enough, they fixed upon plain Ulysses Grant to act the part of Cæsar. It would have been hard to find one less fitted for the rôle. When we look back and contrast what really happened with what the well-read spectators thought was happening, we are reminded of the remark of the British matron to her husband as they left the theatre where they had been seeing the play of "Antony and Cleopatra," "How unlike the home life of our dear Queen!"

The great thing, as President Roosevelt has often reminded us, is to "think nationally." This is no small achievement. A nation is a psycho-geographical fact which it requires a very great effort of the imagination to conceive. The same

word represents a land and the people who in-
habit it. The physical features of the landscape
have their spiritual counterparts. It may be that
the landscape impresses itself on the imagination
of the race, or, as may be maintained with equal
plausibility, the imagination of a gifted race may
interpret the landscape and impress itself upon it
forever. In either case there is a recognizable harmony between the two elements. In reading the
great literature of Israel we never forget that the
nation was desert-born. "He found him in a
desert place, he led him about, he instructed him."
In psalm and prophecy we are conscious of barren mountain ranges, of rocks in a weary land, of
narrow valleys which laugh for very joy over the
incongruity between themselves and the surrounding desolations. There is the passion of the desert,
born of solitude and the stars. In the prophet of
righteousness there is the same urgent note that
Bayard Taylor catches in his "Bedouin Song:"—

> From the Desert I come to thee
> On a stallion shod with fire ;
> And the winds are left behind
> In the speed of my desire.

The impatient human cry is followed by the re-

frain natural to those whose lives are surrounded
by the eternal calm of the desert, —

> Till the sun grows cold,
> And the stars are old,
> And the leaves of the Judgment Book unfold.

When we think of the Greeks we think at the
same time of

> the sprinkled isles
> Lily on lily that o'erlace the sea,
> And laugh their pride when the light wave lisps "Greece."

England and her Englishmen are forever inseparable. "This happy breed of men" belong to
"this little world, this precious stone set in a silver
sea, this blessed plot, this England." That Great
Britain is an island is more than a fact of physical
geography. It is the outward and visible sign of
an insularity of sentiment which gives its peculiar quality to British patriotism. There is something snug and homelike about it, as of a family
that enjoys "the tumultuous privacy of storm."

We become conscious of Spain and her Span-
iards as we read Longfellow's lines : —

> A something sombre and severe
> O'er the enchanted landscape reigned,
> As if King Philip listened near
> And Torquemada, the austere,
> His ghostly sway maintained.

When we come to the United States of America there is a peculiar difficulty in thinking and feeling nationally, because the imagination does not at once find the physical facts to serve as symbols. It is not easy to conceive the land as a whole. When we sing "My Country, 't is of thee," the country that is visualized is very small. The author of the hymn was a New England clergyman, and naturally enough described New England and called it America. It is a land of rocks and rills and woods, and the hills are templed, in Puritan fashion, by white meeting-houses; for the early New Englander, like erring Israel of old, loved to worship on "the high places." Over it all is one great tradition: it is the "land of the Pilgrims' pride."

The farmer in North Dakota loves his country, too; but the idea that it is a land of rocks and rills and templed hills seems to him rather far-fetched. His heart does not thrill with rapture when he thinks of these things. He can plow all day in the Red River valley without striking a stone, and he is glad to have it so.

The Texan cultivates an exuberant Americanism, but he does not think of his country as the

" land of the Pilgrims' pride." Texas is not proud
of the Pilgrims, and perhaps the Pilgrims would
not have appreciated Texas.

When the American has come to feel, not pro-
vincially, but nationally, the words " my country "
bring to his mind not merely some familiar scenes
of his childhood, but a series of vast pictures.
They are broad and simple in outline. " My
country " is no tight little island shut out from
" the envy of less happier lands." It is continental
in its sweep. It lies open and free to all. It is
large and easy of access. There is a vision of
busy cities serving as its gateways. Behind them
is a pleasant home-like land with " a sweet interchange of hill and valley." Beyond the mountains another scene opens. We see the sources of
the strength of America and feel the promise of
its future. To see the Mississippi valley is to believe in " manifest destiny," and to take a cheerful
view of it. To the ancient world the valley of the
Nile was the symbol of fertility. It is a narrow
ribbon of green in the midst of the desert. Here
Plenty and Famine were in plain sight of one
another. There was always the suggestion of
Pharaoh's ugly dream of the lean kine devouring

the fat and well-favored. But in the valley of the Mississippi the fear of the lean kine is dispelled. One may travel at railroad speed day after day, and still the fields of wheat and corn smile upon him. Here the ample land gives happy confidence to men's prayer for daily bread. And beyond the fertile prairies "my country" stretches in high plains and lofty mountain ranges. Here are new treasures waiting bold spirits who claim them. The land has a challenge and an invitation.

> What a weary dearth
> Of the homes of men! What a wild delight
> Of space, of room! What a sense of seas
> Where seas are not! What salt-like breeze!
> What dust and taste of quick alkali!

And beyond the mountains lies the American Avilion, where never —

> wind blows loudly; but it lies
> Deep-meadow'd, happy, fair with orchard lawns
> And bowery hollows: crown'd with summer seas.

And this great land is one; though it is "a nation of nations" it has achieved a national consciousness. There is an atmosphere about it all which we recognize. To breathe it is an exhilaration.

One loves to think of it as the land of "the large and charitable air."

The conception of the continental proportions of America did not at once dawn upon its new inhabitants. They thought and spoke as transplanted Englishmen. Each of the thirteen States was a tight little republic insisting on its own rights. Each plucky Diogenes sat in its own tub, saying to its neighbors, "Get out of my sunshine!"

It was only as they turned westward that Americans discovered America, — a discovery which in some instances has been long delayed. "The West" is not merely a geographical expression, it is a state of mind which is most distinctive of the national consciousness. It is a feeling, an irresistible impulse. It is the sense of undeveloped resources and limitless opportunities. It is associated with the verb "to go." To the American the West is the natural place to go to, as the East is the place to come from. It is synonymous with freedom from restraint. It is always "out West."

Just where the geographical West begins it is

not necessary to indicate. On the coast of Maine you may be shown a summer cottage and told that it belongs to a rich Westerner from Massachusetts. Massachusetts is not thought of as exactly the Far West, but it is far enough.

The psychological West begins at the point where the centre of interest suddenly shifts from the day before yesterday to the day after to-morrow. Great expectations are treated with the respect that elsewhere had been reserved for accomplished facts. There is a stir in the air as if Humanity were a new family just setting up housekeeping. What a fine house it is, and how much room there is on the ground floor! What a great show it will make when all the furniture is in! There is no time now for the finishing touches, but all will come in due order. There is need for unskilled labor and plenty of it. Let every able-bodied man lend a hand.

One does not know his America until he has been touched by the Western fever. He must be possessed by a desire to take up a claim and build himself a shack and invest in a corner lot in a Future Great City. He must be capable of a disinterested joy in watching the improvements

which other people are making. Let the man of
the East cling to the old ways and seek out the
old landmarks. The symbol of the West is the
plank sidewalk leading out from a brand-new
prairie town and pointing to a thriving suburb
which as yet exists only in the mind of its projec-
tor. There is something prophetic in that sidewalk on which the foot of man has never trod.

One who has once had this fever never completely recovers. Though he may change his environment he is always subject to intermittent
attacks.

I remember on my first evening in Oxford
sitting blissfully on the top of a leisurely tram car
that trundled along High Street. The dons in
academic garb were on their way to dinner in the
college halls, and they looked just as my imagination had pictured them. I was introduced to one
of them. When he learned that I was an American, there was a sudden thaw in his manner.

" Have you ever been in Dodge City, Kansas?"
he inquired eagerly.

I modestly replied that I had only passed
through on the railway, but I was familiar with
other Kansas towns, and, reasoning from analogy,

I could tell what manner of place it was. This was enough. I had experienced the West. I was one of the initiated. I could enter into that state of mind represented by the term Dodge City. It appeared that in the golden age, when he and Dodge City were both young, he had sought his fortune for some months in Kansas. He had experienced the joys of civic newness, a newness such as had not been in England since the Heptarchy. He discoursed of the mighty men of those days when every man did what was right in his own eyes, and good-humoredly allowed his neighbor to do likewise. As we parted, he said, with mournful acquiescence in his present estate, " Oxford does very well, you know, but it is n't Dodge City." If poetry is emotion remembered in tranquillity, what could be more poetical than Dodge City remembered in the tranquillity of Oxford quadrangles ?

In this case the poetical view was a sound one. The traveler across the newly developed States of the West has the traveler's license to contrast unfavorably that which he sees with that which he left behind him in his home country. He may say a dozen uncomplimentary things, and each one of them may be true. He may exhaust all his stock adjectives, as "crude" and "raw" and the like. But when he remarks, as did a certain critic, that because the country lacks "distinction" it is uninteresting, he betrays his own limitations.

It is just that lack of distinction that makes America interesting. Here, no longer distracted by what is exceptional, one may take the welfare of the masses of men seriously.

Here the doings of men correspond to the broad doings of the day and the night,
Here is what moves in magnificent masses, careless of particulars.

When Shelley was an undergraduate he was attracted to a lecture on mineralogy. It seemed to him a subject full of poetical suggestiveness. His expectations were disappointed, and he unceremoniously bolted and returned to his room. "What do you think the man talked about? Stones! — stones! — stones! I tell you stones are not interesting — in themselves."

Shelley was right. Stones are not interesting in themselves; neither are railroads, nor stockyards, nor new unpainted buildings, nor endless cornfields. But for that matter, neither are crumbling columns, nor old manuscripts, nor the remains of feudal castles interesting — in themselves. Things become interesting only when seen in relation to the people whose thoughts they have stimulated and whose imaginations they have stirred.

America is a fresh field for human endeavor. Here are men busily making roads, bridging rivers, building new cities. They have been given the task of subduing a continent. But in such conflicts with Nature the conquered influences the conquerors. What impress does the continent make upon the minds of the hardy men who are mastering it ? What visions of the future do they see which transform their drudgery into an heroic adventure ?

In the case of the older nations such questions about the beginnings and the ideals of the beginners cannot be answered. The formative period, with all its significant aspirations, is buried in oblivion. " Who thinks any more as they thought ? " we ask in regard to the pioneer of Britain. Poetry has license to picture him as a knight in armor and to tell how in romantic fashion he pitched

> His tents beside the forest. And he drave
> The heathen, and he slew the beast, and felled
> The forest, and let in the sun.

It was all a long time ago, and the men who did these things are not clearly revealed. Not being able to get at their ideals, we attribute to them those which we think appropriate.

The historians are troubled by their lack of authentic material. They are like the magicians, astrologers, sorcerers, and Chaldeans of the court of Nebuchadnezzar. Nebuchadnezzar had a dream that he knew was very important, but before he could get it interpreted by his wise men he forgot what it was. They were good at interpretations, and could have made one to fit if only the king had brought the dream with him so that they could try it on. But that was the very thing he could not do.

The founders of London and Paris had doubtless their dreams of the future; but alas! they have long since been forgotten. But Chicago has not had time to forget. Everything is still vivid. Men walk the streets of the great city who remember it when it was no bigger than the Londinium of the time of the Cæsars. They have with their own eyes watched every step in the civic development and they have been a part of all that they have seen. The Londoner has seen only a passing phase of his London; the greater part of its history is received on hearsay evidence. The Chicagoan sees his Chicago steadily and sees it whole. No wonder that there is a self-consciousness about the new metropolis that is not to be found in the old. Its greatness has been thrust upon it suddenly, and there is a full realization of its value.

The genuine American who is the maker of the new fortunes of the world, and who is in love with his work, has not been adequately portrayed in literature. It requires an ample imagination to do justice to his character. There must be a mingling of realism and romance. The realism must not be the minute, painstaking portraiture of a Miss Austen, but the hearty, out-of-door reality of a Fielding. The American Fielding has not yet appeared, but what a good time he will have when he comes! What a host of characters after his own heart he will find! The American Scott, too, is called for to give us a story of American life which will read as well on the edge of a clearing in the forest as "The Lady of the Lake" did in the trenches of Torres Vedras, when the soldiers forgot the enemy's shells as they gave a glorious shout over the poet's lines, which their captain was reading to them. I like that story, in spite of the fact that a recent critic declares that to like it shows an uncultivated taste. "This is not," he says, "a test of poetry. An audience less likely to be critical, a situation less likely to induce criticism, can hardly be imagined." Nevertheless, Scott would much rather have written lines that rang true to soldiers in the hour of battle, than to have been given a high mark by the most competent corrector of daily themes.

The imagination of Hawthorne, brooding over the past, repeopled the House of the Seven Gables with the successive generations. But there is another kind of romance, in which the imagination is projected into the future. Looking at the new house not yet enclosed against the storm, it dreams dreams and sees visions. There is a story there, also, and the best of it is that it is to be continued.

A shrewd old New England farmer recounted to me the warlike exploits of his family. He himself had been in Gettysburg, and each generation since the time of the French and Indian wars had had its soldier. His son had been shot at Santiago.

"The bullet went clean through his body," he said, indicating a course which seemed to me necessarily fatal. I expressed sympathy. "Oh, it did n't hurt him much," he said, "it seemed to go through a vacant spot."

That there are vacant spots in the character of the typical man of the Western world no one would be more ready to admit than he. His shortcomings are obvious. Yet most of those which have been harshly commented upon by the world are of the kind that might be commended to the consideration of the kindly Pardoner. Some of his weaknesses touch upon nobleness. Those who best know his environment and the work he has done are most ready to grant him a reasonable degree of indulgence.

The most serious charges against him are that he is a boastful materialist enamored of crude bulk, and that he has trampled upon the old sanctities and is a worshiper of the almighty dollar. There is some color for these charges in his manners, but those who make them have certainly not understood his spirit. "The Western Goth," Lowell called him. The Goths had a bad reputation once as wanton destroyers of ancient art. But after they had had their fling and had settled down, the Teutonic barbarians showed that they could make a thing or two themselves. Gothic has long since ceased to be a term of reproach. Even in the destruction of the ancient, archæologists now admit that the Goths did not do as much harm as was at first feared. The real destroyers of ancient Rome have been the Romans.

From the fact that western America is a place where people are actively engaged in making money, and that they find their work so interesting that they like to talk about it, the superficial observer jumps at the conclusion that this is the seat of the cult of wealth-worship. But there is a vast difference between making a thing and worshiping it. It is reported that one of the varied industries of Great Britain is the manufacture of molten images. It is undoubtedly a sin, but the British manufacturer comforts himself with the reflection that he only breaks half the commandment; he makes the idol, but he does not bow down before it.

Worship is not talkative or boastful. It is reserved and self-abasing. The worshiper accepts the superiority of the object of his devotion as a fact not to be questioned. For such serious-minded worship of wealth go to the English moral tales so popular a generation or two ago, before the wave of democracy came in. Then the afflu-ent Squire and his lady were lifted into the place of superior beings. They dispensed bounty after the manner of Providence to their poorer neigh-bors, and there was no thought of questioning their ways. They were rich, as had been their fathers and mothers before them, and all other virtues were attributed to them by fond superstition.

The men of the Western mining camps, where millionaires are made in a day, have no concep-tion of such a reverential attitude toward the pos-sessor of wealth. When you see them in the eager pursuit of dollars, you are watching not their re-ligion, but their sport. They care for money as the fox-hunter cares for the fox. They admire the man who wins the prize, in proportion to the skill and pluck which he has exhibited. But there are no illusions of a personal superiority imparted by the possession of property. That is impossible in a community where everybody is acquainted with the short and simple annals of the rich.

The man who is conspicuously successful in

the national sport is undoubtedly an object of interest, but it is interest of the superficial sort. He is not the man whom the people delight to honor, and he usually has the good sense to know it. In a Western newspaper my attention was attracted by the headlines : " Noah a Millionaire." It seems that some one had calculated that, even after making allowance for the low price of labor and materials in his day, the Ark must have cost over half a million dollars, and that Noah must have had at least a million in order prudently to undertake the work. It put the patriarch in a fresh light, and I read the article diligently, as did most of my fellow passengers on the train. But that was the end of it; our opinions about diluvian and antediluvian matters remained unchanged. I suppose that the publicity given to the doings of our conspicuously rich contemporaries has no greater significance.

The millionaire who cares for the admiration of his fellow-citizens must do more than accumulate. When he has made his fortune the next question is, " What will he do with it ? " He must do something or sink into the rank of nobodies. Even the most selfish and parsimonious feels that something is required of him. A great part of the stream of new wealth may be wasted, so far as the higher interests of society are concerned, but a certain part of it is pretty certain to be directed toward those same higher interests. The process is like that which goes on with an hydraulic ram. Where there is a good stream of water, one can afford to lose most of it. The waste water, before it escapes down the hill, pumps a slender but sufficient stream into the second story.

Indeed, it is the interest of our millionaires in art, science, and religion which has created a puzzling ethical problem. They are not content to be mere money-getters. They aspire to be benefactors on a large scale. But what if the wealth so freely offered has not been honestly come by? What if the best institutions should hesitate to receive it? The poor rich man cannot contemplate such a refusal with equanimity. It would interfere with the fulfillment of his most cherished plans. To have unlimited opportunities to make money, and to be hindered in giving it away, seems to him like building a trunk line of railroad and then being denied terminal facilities. Of course he could change his plans and keep it all himself, but to a man who had been accustomed to " doing things " that would be a humiliating anti-climax.

The fact that the American is greatly absorbed in his work with material things is no sufficient basis of the charge of materialism that is lightly brought against him. The crucial question is, " What do the things stand for in his mind? Are they finalities, or are they means to an end ? " The most appalling picture of a purely materialistic civilization is that given in the book of the Revelation. It is an inventory of the wealth of the Babylon which was Imperial Rome. The inventory is an indictment. " The merchandise of gold, and silver, and precious stones, and of pearls, and fine linen, and purple, and silk, and scarlet, and all thyine wood, and all manner vessels of ivory, and all manner vessels of most precious wood, and of brass, and iron, and marble, and cinnamon, and odours, and ointments, and frankincense, and wine, and oil, and fine flour, and wheat, and beasts, and sheep, and horses, and chariots, and slaves, and souls of men."

The heart grows sick when the list of commodities ends with the "souls of men." What were they worth, measured against all that goes before ?

A very different impression comes as we read Joaquin Miller's exultant cry over the West : —

> O heart of the world's heart, West! my West!
> Look up! Look out! There are fields of kine,
> There are clover fields that are red as wine,
> . . . .
> There are emerald seas of corn and cane,
> . . . .
> There are isles of oak and a harvest plain
> Where brown men bend to the bending grain,
> There are temples of God and towns new born.
> . . . .
> And the hearts of oak and the hands of horn
> Have fashioned them all, and a world beside.

This frank delight in the riches of the earth is not materialistic. The souls of men are not in the market. They form the supreme standard of value. Materialism is not a disease to which nations are subject in their lusty youth. It comes with senile decay.

Sometimes when we are wearied with the intense activity of modern life we quote the saying, " Things are in the saddle." Perhaps our sympathy is misplaced. If the poor Things could speak, they would tell us that, so far from being in the saddle, they are under the lash of furious young

idealists who give them no rest. It is the nature of
a Thing to "stay put," but these headstrong youths
despise this conservative bias. They are no respect-
ers of Things, being wholly absorbed in Purposes.

To see Things in undisputed possession, go into
"the best room" of a respectable old farmhouse.
Here the Thing has the place of honor, and the
Person is a base intruder, having no rights of his
own. The priestess hovers occasionally around
her sacred Things, waving her feather duster as a
mystic wand, and then leaves them in respectful
gloom. Nothing short of a death in the family
would induce her to disturb them. Go into a busy
workshop, and you may see how the Thing may
be taught to know its place. It is always at the
mercy of the innovating Intelligence. When a
new Idea comes, the old Thing which had heretofore had a useful function is thrown aside. It is
still as good as it ever was, but it is not good
enough. It must go to the scrap pile.

The man of the West is likely to offend against
the standards of propriety in speech. When he
begins to explain the character of his country, he
is accused of inaccuracy. His prospectus is not

always confirmed by the Table of Contents. He has acquired the habit of "talking large." This prejudices many people against him. They accuse him of willful exaggeration, and if he be the promoter of some commercial enterprise, they impute to him a mercenary motive.

But he is in reality quite sincere. If he talks large, it is only because he feels large. His is a language natural to those who are engaged in creative work, and who foresee great things. It is like "the large utterance of the early gods." He does not feel called upon to limit his statements to the facts that are already apparent; he expects the facts to grow up to his statements. He is not shooting at a fixed target, but at a flying mark; if he is to hit it, he must aim a little ahead.

Another reason for this large utterance is that in a new country the ordinary man identifies himself with his community in a way impossible to any but very great magnates in an old civilization. He feels very much as did the kings and earls he has read about. How proudly on the Shakespearean stage a great noble will speak of himself as Norfolk or Northumberland! It is as if his personality had been multiplied by so many square miles. He is no longer a mere individual, — he is a whole county.

An American may have much the same sense of territorial aggrandizement by identifying himself with a promising community in its first stage of growth. He is not a unit lost in a multitude. His town has a fine name and a glorious future. Some day these glories may be divided among thousands, now they are his own. He is proud of the town, and the pride is more satisfying because he is it.

I once camped for a whole month in the city of Naples on the shores of the Pacific. I knew it was a city, for a huge sign announced the fact to every one who passed by the beautiful, secluded spot. Unlike some of the boom towns of that period, Naples had an inhabitant, whom I had occasion frequently to meet. When I addressed him, it was hard for me to use his surname, as I would with a common man. For to me he was Naples. It would have seemed appropriate for him to speak in blank verse.

There are those who look upon the Western delight in the idea of bigness as an evidence of vulgarity of sentiment and of the lack of idealism. They have a scorn of those who habitually think of quantity rather than of quality. But the man of fastidious taste should not be allowed to have it all his own way. One poet may be inspired by "the murmur of a hidden brook in the leafy month of June." But another may prefer to stand on the shore of the ocean and feel its immensity. He is tremendously impressed by its size. It is a big thing. But the ocean is as poetical as the brook, though in its own huge way.

There are some things wherein quality is the first consideration. They are the luxuries of life. But when we come to the prime necessities, the first question is in regard to the adequacy of the supply. When a sentimental young lady was seated at dinner next to a great poet, she waited, awestruck, for him to give utterance to a fine thought. The only gem he vouchsafed was, "How do you like your mutton? I like mine in hunks." The poet was a man of sound sense. There is one law for poetry and another for mutton. Poetry is precious, and a little goes a long way; we can get on without any but the best. But mutton should be served more generously.

It is the glory of the West that it treats what elsewhere are the luxuries of the few as the necessities of the many. It dispenses even "the higher education" not in dainty morsels, but in hunks.

Old Mrs. Means, in "The Hoosier Schoolmaster," formulated the wisdom of the pioneer. "You see, this 'ere bottom land was all Congress land in them there days and sold for a dollar and a quarter, and I says to my old man, 'Jack,' says I, 'do you git a plenty while you 're gittin'. Git a plenty while you 're gittin',' says I, 'for 't wont be no cheaper than 't is now;' and it haint, and I knowed 't would n't."

Translate Mrs. Means's shrewd maxim into the terms of idealism, and you have the characteristic contribution of the West. The old prudential maxims, which were true enough in a finished civilization, may well be disregarded by those who face a great new opportunity. They can well afford to preëmpt more territory than they can at present cultivate. When one's aims are selfish, the desire to get a plenty is mere greed, but in the altruist it rises into "the enthusiasm for humanity." It is the ambition to supply the wants of men no longer in niggardly fashion, but in full measure.

In two directions the expectation of moral amplitude in things American is fulfilled, — in Education and in Charity. Here we feel that the people have been aroused to the need of making plentiful provision, not only for immediate necessities, but for future growth. Along these lines we think and plan nationally.

But there are some questions which give pause to the most boastful patriot. Where is the distinctive American Art which interprets in a broad, fresh way the genius of the land, and where is the public that would recognize it and delight in it if it should appear? Where is the great American Church able splendidly to organize the forces of spiritual freedom as Rome organized the principles of ecclesiastical authority? How is the vision of her prophets fulfilled?

> And thou, America,
> For the scheme's culmination, its thought and its reality,
> For these (not for thyself) thou hast arrived.
> Thou, too, surroundest all,
> Embracing, carrying, welcoming all, thou too by pathways
>   broad and new,
> To the ideal tendest.

The measured faiths of other lands, the grandeurs of the past
Are not for thee, but grandeurs of thine own,
Deific faiths and amplitudes, absorbing, comprehending all.

Where are these "deific faiths and amplitudes" that are worthy of the land embodied?

America presents new problems for statesmanship; where are the large-hearted, clear-eyed men who give themselves to the task? Here and there we see them. In the crisis of the nation's life nature came to the rescue.

For him her Old-World moulds aside she threw,
And, choosing sweet clay from the breast
Of the unexhausted West,
With stuff untainted shaped a hero new,
Wise, steadfast in the strength of God, and true.

That is the kind of manhood America needs. Is the supply equal to the demand? The growth of wealth in the Republic has been marvelous. Has there been evolved a wisdom equal to the task of justly distributing what enterprise has created? We hear of American "Captains of Industry." How far have they realized Carlyle's idea when he gave the title to those whose success lies not in personal gain but in ability to be real leaders of men? How far has America produced great captains, able to bring into commerce and manufacture the soldierly virtues of courage, loyalty, and willing obedience?

When he considers these things the just critic must say to the Republic, "Thou art weighed in the balances and found wanting." But let him not hastily assume that he is reading the mystic handwriting on the wall, the *Mene, mene, tekel, upharsin,* that foretells the fall of nations. Let him rather talk as to a young athlete who has not come up to the mark, "You have done much, but you have not yet done your best! You are yet wanting in some essential elements. You must try again."

The American idealist recognizes the present failures, but it does not quench his high spirits. They come to him as challenges. He takes his falls as Adam and Eve took theirs. After the first shock was over there was a healthy reaction.

> Some natural tears they dropped, but wiped them soon;
> The world was all before them where to choose
> Their place of rest, and Providence their guide.

The most hopeful sign of the times is the number of young Americans who have become conscious of the grave evils that beset their country.

but who neither whine nor scold nor prophesy ill. The pioneer spirit is strong within them. They attack the abuses of democracy with a cheery iconoclasm. They are impelled to their work not merely by a sense of duty; they find their fun in it. It is with a sense of exhilaration that we watch these pioneers. Their world is all before them. We are anxious to see what they will make of it.

A COMMUNITY OF HUMORISTS

HUMOR is not usually looked upon as a civic virtue. It is for the most part confined to a modest sphere of usefulness, and is accepted as an alleviation to the lot of the private man. He learns to find pleasure in his small misadventures and to smile amiably at his discomfitures. The most ancient pleasantries have almost always an element of domesticity. They form the silver lining to the clouds that sometimes gather over the most peaceful homes. What comfort an ancient Hebrew must have taken in the text from Ecclesiasticus: "As climbing up a sandy way is to the feet of the aged, so is a wife full of words to a quiet man." The quiet man would murmur to himself, "How true!" He would seize the simile as a dog snatches a bone, and would carry it off to enjoy it by himself.

But it would never occur to him to treat the large affairs of the community in this fashion. Here everything seems too dignified to allow of pleasant conceits. The quiet man could not treat the prolixity of his social superiors as he could the too long drawn out wisdom of his wife. He must take it, as he would take the invariable laws of nature, with unsmiling acquiescence. Lord Bacon in his list of works that ought to be undertaken declared the need of one to be entitled " Sober Satire ; or the Insides of Things." Such sober satire might express the moods of a philosophical statesman, who could contrast the inside of great affairs with the outside. It implies a certain familiarity with the institutions of society which the common man does not possess.

Now and then, however, there is a reversal of the usual relation. The community is of such a nature that each member can see through it and all around it. The ordinary citizen becomes a philosopher indulging habitually in sober satire. He knows that things are not as they seem, and is pleased at the discovery. In such a case humor envelops everything and becomes the last word of sociological wisdom.

So it was in a community which I fondly remember. It was not much to look at, this brand-new Nevada mining town. The main street swaggered up the gulch in a devil-may-care fashion, as if saying to the teamsters, " You may take me or leave me." To the north it pointed to an alkali flat, and to the south to a dusty old mountain, which was immensely richer than it seemed. On the mountain side were hoisting works and hundreds of prospect holes which menaced the lives of the unwary. In the gulch were smelters which belched forth divers kinds of fumes. To the stranger they seemed to threaten wholesale asphyxiation, but to the citizen they gave the place the character of a health resort. An analysis of the air showed that it contained more chemicals than were to be found in the most famous mineral springs. Certain it was that there were enough to kill off all germs of contagious diseases. The community felt the need of no further hygienic precautions, and put its trust in its daily fumigations. No green thing was in sight, not so much as a grass blade, for the fumes were not only germicides, but also herbicides. On the main street were saloons and gambling houses, in close proximity to two or three struggling churches. There were two daily newspapers, each of which kept us informed of the other's manifold iniquities. A narrow-gauge railroad had its terminus at the foot of the gulch. Once a day a mixed train would depart for the world that lay beyond the alkali flat. Some of the passengers would be "going below," which meant nothing worse than a trip to California; others were promoters going East on missions of mercy to benighted capitalists. The promoter was our nearest approach to a professional philanthropist. As for the rest, the chief impression was of dust. It would roll in great billows down the gulch; it seemed as if the mountains had been pulverized. Then the wind would change and the dust billows would roll back. No matter how long it blew, there was always more where it came from.

I cannot explain to an unsympathetic reader why it was that we found life in our dusty little metropolis so charming, and why it was that we felt such pity for those who had never experienced the delights of our environment. Nor can I justify to such a reader the impulse which led a woman whose husband had died far away in New England to bring his body back to be laid to rest in the bare little cemetery amid the sage brush.

"It's not such a homelike country as the other,"
I ventured.

"No," she answered, "it isn't, but he liked it."

And so did we all; and the liking was not the
less real because it was an acquired taste. There
was nothing in it akin to serious public spirit.
It was a whimsical liking, like that of Touch-
stone for Audrey, — "An ill-favoured thing, sir,
but mine own; a poor humour of mine, sir, to
take that that no man else will."

When several thousand people, set down in
the midst of a howling wilderness, tacitly agree
to consider it as the garden of the Lord, they can
do much. It pleases the ephemeral community
to make believe that it is permanent. The camp
organizes itself into a city, with all the offices and
dignities appertaining thereto. Civilization is
extemporized like a game of dumb crambo. It
amuses the citizens to see their beloved city going
about in institutions several sizes too large for it.
Nothing is taken literally. Humor is accepted
not as a private possession, but as a public trust,
and cultivated in a spirit of generous coöpera-
tion.

In the town were men whose education and

experience had been in the great world. There were mine superintendents who a little while ago might have been in Germany or Cornwall; there were assayers and engineers fresh from the great technical schools, and "experts" full of geological lore. The mines were as rich in litigation as in silver, and there were lawyers great and small.

But all were dominated by one typical character who was accepted as the oracle of the land, — "The Honest Miner." To him saloons were dedicated with alluring titles, such as "The Honest Miner's Delight" and "The Honest Miner's Rest." At the end of the gulch was "The Honest Miner's Last Chance," — one which he seldom missed. The newspapers and political orators appealed to his untutored judgments as the last word of political wisdom. He occupied the position which elsewhere is held by the "Sturdy Yeoman" or the "Solid Business Man."

The Honest Miner of the Far West is one of those typical Americans who are builders of commonwealths. His impress is upon the western half of our continent. He is a nomad, the last of a long line of adventurers to whom the delight

of the new world is in its newness. Sometimes
his work is permanent, but he never is quite
sure. His habitual mood is one of sober satire.

I know nothing more pleasant than to sit with
an old-timer who has spent years in prospecting
for silver and gold, and listen to his reminiscences.
Here is a philosopher indeed, one with an historic
perspective. He has the experience of the Wandering Jew, without his world-weariness. He has
seen the rise and fall of cities and the successive
dynasties of mining kings. His life has been a
mingling of society and solitude. With his pack
upon his back he has wandered into desert places
where no man had been since the making of
the world, — at least, no man with an eye to the
main chance. A few weeks later the lonely cañon
has become populated with eager fortune-seekers.
The camp becomes a city which to the eyes of
the Honest Miner is one of the wonders of the
world. A year later he revisits the scene, and
it is as Tadmor in the Wilderness. He pauses to
refresh his mind with ancient history, and then
passes on to join in a new "excitement." He
measures time by these excitements as the Greeks
measured it by Olympiads.

He loves to tell of the ups and downs of his own fortune. There is no bitterness in his memory of his failures. They relieve the record from the monotony that belongs to assured success. His successes are not less gratifying because, like all things earthly, they have had a speedy ending. A dozen times he has " struck it rich." He has thrown away his pick and shovel and gone below to bask in the smiles of fortune. He has indulged in vague dreams of going to Europe, of looking up his family tree, and of cultivating grammar and other fine arts. Fortune continued to smile, but after a while her smile became sardonic, and with a wink she said, " Time's up ! " Then the Honest Miner would take up his pick and shovel and return to his work, neither a sadder nor a wiser man, — in fact, exactly the same kind of man he was before. That Experience is a teacher is a pedantic theory which he rejects with scorn. Experience is not a schoolmaster, Experience is a chum who likes to play practical jokes upon him. Just now he has given him a tumble and got the laugh on him. But just wait awhile ! And he chuckles to himself as he thinks how he will outwit Experience.

All the traditions of the mining country confirm him in his point of view: Listen to what Experience says, and then do just the opposite. It is the unexpected that happens. The richest diggings bear the most lugubrious names. The Montanian delights to tell of the riches taken out of Last Chance Gulch. The Arizonian for years boasted of the gayety of Tombstone and the amazing prosperity of the Total Wreck Mine.

Certain physiologists are now telling us that the poetic praise of wine is based upon a mistake. Alcohol, they say, is not a stimulant, but a depressant. It does not stimulate the imagination so much as it depresses the critical faculty so that dullness may easily pass for wit. An idea will occur to a sober man as being rather bright, but before he has time to express it he sees that it is not so. Under the inhibition of good sense he holds his tongue and saves his reputation. But in a convivial company the inhibition is removed. Everybody says whatever is uppermost in his mind. The mice play, not because they are more lively than before, but only because the cat is away.

On first hearing this theory, it seemed to me

that it was the most powerful temperance argument which could be formulated. But I am not sure but that it leaves the matter very much where it found it. After all, the man who is oppressed by the dullness of his ordinary condition would enjoy feeling brilliant, even if he were not really so.

In trying to recall any specific instances of wit and humor in my Nevada town, I am compelled to fall back on the theory of the removal of inhibition. Life was not more amusing there than elsewhere, — it only seemed so. There were no " best people " whose critical judgments inhibited the self-expression of less favored classes. Every one feeling at liberty to be himself and to express his own opinion, unfailing variety was assured. Society, being composed of all sorts and conditions of men, was in a state of perpetual effervescence. A very ordinary man, who elsewhere might have passed unnoticed in a life of drudgery, became a notable character.

There, for example, was Old Multitude, so called from the many oxen attached to the huge wagons he convoyed to the distant mines. He was a bull-whacker of the old school. His surname had long been lost in the abyss of time. Old Multitude was not looked upon as a mere individual. The public had adopted him, and he had become an institution.

When he was about to depart, a crowd would gather on the main street, as the inhabitants of a little seaport town gather to watch the departure of a ship. Old Multitude bore his honors meekly, but he was conscious that he was the chief actor in an important social function. There was nothing ill-advised in his actions, and his words were fitly chosen as he walked down the line, addressing to each beast of his multitudinous team the appropriate malediction. His wide vocabulary on such occasions contrasted strangely with his usual taciturnity. The words taken by themselves were blood-curdling enough, but as they rose and fell in mighty undulations it seemed as if he were intoning a liturgy.

And there was Old Tansy, a bit of wreckage from the times of '49. There was a tradition that Tansy had seen better days; at least, it was hard to imagine how he could have seen worse. He lived without visible means of support, and yet he was not submerged. It pleased the community to accept Tansy as a character worth knowing in spite of his fallen fortunes. His obvious failings were always clothed in soft euphemisms. No one could say that he had ever seen him drunk, and on the other hand no one would be so rash as to assert that he had ever seen him sober. In the border land between moderate drinking and inebriety, Tansy dwelt in peace.

What most endeared Tansy to his fellows was his mild religiosity, which manifested itself in persistent church-going. He was no fair-weather Christian. There was no occasion when he would not desert his favorite saloon to take his accustomed place in the back pew of the Presbyterian church. Only once did Tansy express an opinion in regard to the services which he so assiduously attended. A minister passing through the town preached a lurid sermon on the future punishment of the wicked. He spared no materialistic imagery to make his remarks effective. At the close of the service Tansy, instead of going out, as was his custom, went forward and, grasping the minister's hands, said in a tone of quiet satisfaction, " Parson, it done me good."

Just what the nature of the good was he did

not indicate. I suppose that there was something in the unction of the preacher that recalled memories of the past.

There was one person whom I always recall with peculiar pleasure. To see him coming over the divide in a cloud of dust was to see one of the typical forms of creation. He was known, on account of the huge pair of goggles which he wore, as "Four-Eyed Nick." He dwelt in a cabin in the most desolate part of the mountain, and he fitted his environment perfectly. He seemed as natural a product of the soil as the sage brush, for like it he had learned to exist where there was very little water.

Great was the joy in the community when one day Four-Eyed Nick announced that he had struck pay ore and that he was about to celebrate his good fortune by getting married. Every one was intensely interested. The newspapers made an especial feature of the approaching marriage in high life. Nick was dazed by the sudden glare of publicity. Who should be invited? His generous heart rebelled against any discrimination, and he solved his problem by saying, "Come one! Come all!" He engaged every vehicle in the town to be at the disposal of such of his fellow citizens as would honor him with their presence at his nuptials.

It would have delighted the heart of Chaucer to have seen the procession of wedding guests wending their way over the ten miles of abominable mountain road to Nick's cabin. Not on the road to Canterbury was there more variety or more hearty good fellowship. Nick had invited the town, and the town was bent on showing its appreciation of the compliment. The mayor and members of the city council, the lawyers, editors, doctors, clergymen, gamblers, mining experts, saloon-keepers, and honest miners all joined heartily in doing honor to one whom they, for the moment, agreed to consider their most distinguished fellow citizen.

No one could remain long in assured obscurity. It pleased the community to turn its search-light now upon one member and now upon another, and give him a brief experience of living in the public eye. Greatness of one sort or another was sure to be thrust upon one in the course of the year. The choicest spirits of the town were always collaborating in some work of high-grade fiction, and were on the lookout for interesting material. It would have been churlish for any one when his turn came to have refused to be a notability.

An English writer laments the fact that the schools send out thousands of persons whose imaginations have been stifled by the too prosaic discipline which they have undergone. " Why," he says, " is it that ninety-nine persons out of a hundred lose this faculty in the earliest period of their childhood ? It is simply because their bring-ing up has consisted in the persistent inoculation with the material facts of life, and the correspond-ingly persistent elimination of all imaginative ideas."

He blames parents who give their children mechanical toys, especially if they are well made. Even a doll should not have too much verisim-ilitude. " It would be better to place a bundle of rags in the arms of a little girl, and tell her to imagine it to be a baby. She would, if left to herself with no other resource than her own fancy learn to exercise all her dormant powers of im-agination and originality."

That kind of education the Honest Miner has

carried into mature life. He is full of imaginative ideas. The barest shanty is glorified in his eyes if it bears the sign " Palace Hotel " or " Delmonico's." If he cannot have the thing, he takes satisfaction in the name. Above all else, he craves variety.

The inhabitants of Gold Hill used to relate with pleasure the exploits of Sandy Bowers. When he struck an incredibly rich pocket in the mountain, Sandy built for himself a huge and expensive mansion in Washoe Valley. He imported all kinds of trees from foreign lands, none of which would grow. He filled his house with pianos, and when some one suggested sheet music he telegraphed to New York: "Send me some sheet music, one of every kind."

It was the desire for one of every kind which induced our community, when it put off the habits of a " camp " and became a " city," to lift into temporary prominence an elderly farmer from Pennsylvania who had drifted into Nevada without changing any of his ways. He came from York County, where he would have gone on his way unnoticed, for there were so many like him. But in the silver country he was different

from the common run of fortune-seekers, therefore he was made much of. Some local Diogenes
turned his lantern upon him and discovered that
he was an honest man, honest in a plodding,
Pennsylvania Dutch fashion. "Honest John"
became a man of note. Then some one suggested
that we had "in our midst a grand old man."
That was enough to make the political fortune
of the honest man. He was elected to a position
of power in the new city government, for every
one was anxious to see what our "grand old
man" would do.

He proved a thorn in the flesh of the politicians. He introduced a reign of rigid economy
which made the local statesmen despair of the
Republic. It was decided that the city had had
too much of a good thing. The Grand Old
Man should be deposed, — he should not be
mayor, nor member of the council, nor any such
thing.

But the municipal charter had been conceived
in that generous fashion which is proper to a state
where there are offices in excess of the needs of the
population. The Grand Old Man discovered that
there was one office which had been overlooked

by the astute politicians : that of the Superintendent of Streets and Sidewalks. The streets had
not been clearly differentiated from the surrounding desert, and, as for sidewalks, the citizens had
been accustomed to cut across the country wherever it pleased them. The highways having been
left to the kindly influence of Nature, it never
occurred to any one that they should be officially
superintended. The Grand Old Man cast a ballot
for himself as Superintendent of Streets and Sidewalks, and when the returns were in, it was found
that his name led all the rest. He was declared
elected by a majority of one.

Then he began to magnify his office. He
brought forth a plan of the city which had heretofore been a dead letter. He discovered streets
where the wildest imagination had not supposed
streets to be possible. Prominent citizens were
arrested for obstructing mythical sidewalks. He
was encouraged to stretch his prerogatives to the
utmost, for every one was curious to see how far
they would go. For six months he ruled by right
of eminent domain. Leading lawyers gave it as
their opinion that all rights not expressly reserved
by the Federal and State governments were vested

in the Grand Old Man. The Methodist minister, who was inclined to sensationalism, preached a sermon from the text in Nehemiah vi. 6: "It is reported among the heathen, and Gashmu saith it." "Who this Gashmu was," said the preacher, in beginning his discourse, "we do not know, but from the importance attributed to his remarks we may fairly assume that he was the Superintendent of Streets and Sidewalks in Jerusalem."

Lowell describes the rough humor of the frontier, with the free and easy manners which characterize

> this brown-fisted rough, this shirt-sleeved Cid,
> This back-woods Charlemagne of empires new,
> Whose blundering heel instinctively finds out
> The goutier foot of speechless dignities,
> Who, meeting Cæsar's self, would slap his back,
> Call him 'Old Horse' and challenge to a drink.

He had in mind the backwoodsmen whom sturdy apostles like Peter Cartwright labored with to such good purpose. But the Honest Miner, though a pioneer, is not a backwoodsman. His humor is of a different quality. He would not think of slapping Cæsar on the back and calling him "Old Horse." It would seem more amusing to him to address some one who might properly be called " Old Horse " with titles of honor.

" Truthful James " delights in euphemism. He does not object to calling a spade a spade, but he refuses to do so in such a way as to give offense.

> Which it is not my style
> To produce needless pain
> By statements that rile
> Or that go 'gin the grain.

He is no " brown-fisted rough " who delights in swagger. There is roughness enough all about him, and it pleases him to cultivate the amenities. His gentlemanliness is often carried to excess.

The most characteristic humor of the Honest Miner consists, not in grotesque exaggeration, but in delicate understatement. What can be more considerate than the notice posted by the side of an open shaft: " Gentlemen will please not fall down this shaft, for there are men at work below."

A Nevada minister once described to me the action of a brother minister in the early days. The minister went to a certain town where he offended the lawless element, and was threatened with physical violence if he persisted in his intention of preaching. My friend described the method by which the liberty of prophesying was asserted. " He went into the pulpit, laid his revolver on the Bible — and then he preached *extempore*."

The manner of narration savored of the soil. The Honest Miner under such circumstances would subordinate everything to emphasis on the correct homiletical method. No matter how able the minister might be, it was evident that if he were closely confined to his notes, his delivery could not be effective.

A good woman described the way in which her minister, a young man fresh from the theological school, made one of his first parish calls. He found his parishioner, who had been extolled as one of the pillars of the church, in a state of intoxication, and he was chased out of the house and some distance down the street.

" We were sorry it happened, for it gave him an unpleasant impression of the congregation. You know Mr. —— met with several rebuffs."

The unconventional episode was related with all the prim propriety of " Cranford."

The perfect democracy of a mining camp develops a certain naïve truth-telling, which has
all the unexpectedness which belongs to the
observations of a boy. There is no attempt to
reduce everything to uniformity, or to prove any
particular thesis. The gossip of a conventional
village where people know each other too well
is apt to be malicious. A creditable action is
narrated, and then comes the inevitable "but."
The subject of conversation falls in the estima-
tion of the hearers with a sudden thud.

The Honest Miner does not attempt to pass
final judgment or to arrange his fellow men according to any sort of classification. He speaks
of them as he sees them, and so virtues and failings jostle one another and take no offense. The
result is a moral inconsequence which has all
the effect of studied wit. This is what delights us
in the characterization of Thompson of Angel's:

Frequently drunk was Thompson, but always polite to the
stranger.

As we read the line we smile, not so much at
Thompson as at the society of which he was a
part. We see behind him the sympathetic company at Angel's. Here was a public with whose

temper he was familiar. He could trust himself
to the judgment of his peers. No misdemeanor
would blind them to such virtues as he actually
possessed. He could appeal to them with perfect confidence.

> When you shall these unlucky deeds relate,
> Speak of me as I am; nothing extenuate,
> Nor set down aught in malice.

The Western mining camp is not primarily
an educational institution, yet it has served a
most important function in the making of Americans. The young man is fortunate who on leaving college can take a post-graduate course in
a community where he can study sociology at
first hand. He will learn many things, especially
that human nature is not so simple as it seems,
but that it has many " dips, spurs, and angles."

A SAINT RECANONIZED

"ALL the world loves a lover," but all the world does not love a saint. Our hearts do not leap up when we behold a halo on the title-page, and so the lives of the heroes of the Church are frequently neglected. When the saint has been duly canonized, that is generally the end of him in popular esteem. But sometimes the ecclesiastical and secular judgments coincide and the saint is invested with human interest.

So it has been with St. Francis of Assisi,— given the highest honors in his church, he has captivated the imagination of the world. Protestants vie with Catholics in doing him honor. At no time has his name been more familiar or his legend more often repeated than in our own day. He has been recanonized.

This renewal of interest in the Franciscan legend is all the more interesting because it carries us into a region so remote from that in which we habitually dwell.

"Now it came to pass that as Francis, the servant of the Lord, was singing the praises of the Lord with joy and gladness, certain robbers fell upon him and fiercely questioned him who he was. And he answered, 'I am the herald of the King of Heaven.' And the robbers fell upon him with blows and cast him into a ditch, saying, 'Lie there, thou herald of nothing!' When they had departed Francis arose and went through the forest, singing with a loud voice the praises of the Creator."

These words take us into another world than ours. To enter that world we must not only lay aside our easily besetting sins, but our easily besetting virtues as well. We must cast aside all the prudential virtues, we must rid our minds of all prejudice in favor of scientific charity and rationalistic schemes of philanthropy, and we must disclaim personal responsibility for the progress of modern civilization. With such impedimenta the pilgrim of thought might possibly get as far back as the sixteenth century, but it would be impossible for him to penetrate into the thirteenth. He who would do so must first drink deep of Lethe. He must put out of mind those persons

and events which have been the distinctive influences of the modern world. He must forget
Luther, and wash his soul clean of every trace
of Calvin; every echo of the raillery of Voltaire
must have died away, and his mind must have
been kept unspotted from the world of Newton
and of Darwin.

Above all, if he would enter into the social
dreams of the thirteenth century, he must forget
that he ever heard of such a science as political
economy. He must renounce the old Adam and
all his works, — I mean Adam Smith.

But on the other side of Lethe there are pure
fountains, and dark forests where robbers lurk,
and where saints are singing the high praises of
God, and beyond are the "regions dim of rapture" where they are lost from the eyes of their
disciples.

And it may not be in vain to turn aside from
the consideration of the engrossing questions of
our day, to enter into that dim world and look
out upon it through the eyes of its truest saints.
They were eyes blind to many things we see
clearly, but they saw some things which we do
not always see; at any rate they were eyes —

> Beyond my knowing of them beautiful,
> Beyond all knowing of them wonderful,
> Beautiful in the light of holiness.

So Francis of Assisi has an especial interest for every student of Christianity and for every student of ethics. For the student of Christianity he stands as a man who, while neither a theologian nor a reformer, and having no place among the intellectual leaders of mankind, has an undisputed spiritual leadership. His place is that of the little child whom Jesus placed in the midst and of whom he said, "Of such is the kingdom of Heaven."

For the student of ethics St. Francis is of interest because, while he had an invincible ignorance of scientific ethics, yet the real emphasis of his life and teaching was on the finest kind of ethical idealism. We are reminded of Shakespeare's lines : —

> Love is too young to know what conscience is,
> Yet who knows not that conscience is born of love.

There are some characters, and St. Francis is among them, who belong so completely to their own age that we cannot take them out of their environment. The beauty of their lives is like that of some shy wild flower which will not bear transplanting.   If we would enjoy it we must go where it grows. To appreciate these characters we need not critical knowledge, but imaginative sympathy.

There is an old Irish legend of a young hero who sailed to a far country and married a beautiful princess.   Living there he enjoyed perpetual youth, and three centuries passed away as if they had been but three years.   Then came a longing to return to his own native land.   After much entreating his fair wife allowed him to return on one condition, and that was that he should not dismount from the white steed she gave him. The prince came back, but riding in youthful strength and beauty through the familiar land, at last he forgot the condition. Dismounting, his feet touched the ground, and the enchantment vanished.   Suddenly he realized the passage of time.   His friends, the heroes of his youth, were dead and forgotten. He was very old; his strength had withered away.   The joyous paganism in which he had been bred had been driven away. He saw processions of monks and nuns, and heard the sound of church bells, and saw over all the shadow of the cross. He belonged to the old order that had passed away, now the destinies of the land were in the hands of new men.

Something of this same caution must be used by those who would see the St. Francis whom the people long ago loved and worshiped. He is the embodiment of mediæval goodness. Let us beware of disenchanting literalism, lest suddenly the radiant youth disappear and we see only the relic of an age that has passed away.

Let us not look back at St. Francis. Let us stand at the beginning of the thirteenth century and look forward. Let us share the dream of the youth who went through the forest singing the praise of God.

The transformation of worldly ambition into spiritual was never more vividly told than in the legend of St. Francis, by the Three Companions. We see Francis the gay son of Peter Bernardone, merchant of Assisi, transformed into a knight of Lady Poverty.

" Then a few years later a certain noble of the city of Assisi provided himself with warlike gear to go into Apulia to increase his profit of money and renown. Upon hearing this, Francis did

aspire to go with him and to be made a knight
by a certain count, Gentile by name; wherefore
he made ready stuffs as costly as he could, poorer
in riches than his fellow citizen, but more profuse
in largesse.   One night when he had given all
his thoughts to bringing this to pass, and was
fevered with the desire for making the journey,
he was visited by the Lord, who draweth him as
one eager for glory to the pinnacle of glory by a
vision and uplifteth him.   For while sleeping that
night one appeared unto him, calling him by
name, and leading him into the palace of a fair
bride, very pleasant and full of knightly armor,
to wit, glittering shields and other apparel hanging on the wall as it were waiting for knights to
accoutre them therewithal.   And while he, rejoi-
cing greatly, marveled silently within himself what
this might be, he asked whose were these arms
flashing with such splendor and this so pleasant
palace ?   And the answer was made him that the
palace and all things therein were his own and his
knights'.   And thus awakening with joyous heart
he rose early. . . . And so much gayer than his
wont did he seem that many wondered thereat,
and asked whence had he such joy, unto whom

he would reply, "I know that I shall be a great prince."

It was not the sense of sin that proved the beginning of a new life to this light-hearted Italian. It was rather the sense of a higher chivalry. Another vision came to him. A voice asked, "'Which can do the better for thee, the lord or the servant?'

"And when he answered, 'The lord,' that other said again unto him, 'Wherefore then dost thou leave the lord for the servant, and a rich lord for a poor?' . . . Then waking he began earnestly to ponder this vision. And just as in the first vision he had been, as it were, quite carried out of himself for his great joy, coveting worldly good fortune, so in this vision he withdrew within himself entirely, wondering at its might, and meditating so earnestly that he could sleep no more that night."

At last the new vision took form in an enthusiastic way of life. In the church Francis heard the words of the gospels, "Take no gold nor silver nor money in your purses, nor two coats, nor shoes, nor staff."

No further did he need to listen. Throwing

away his purse, and putting on the garb of a
peasant, he devoted himself henceforth not simply to the service of the poor, but to the worship
of Poverty. Dante in memorable words described
this lover-like devotion.

> For he in youth his father's wrath incurred
> For certain Dame, to whom as unto death
> The gate of pleasure no one doth unlock ;
>
> .   .   .   .
>
> Then day by day more fervently he loved her.
> She reft of her first husband, scorned, obscure,
> One thousand and one hundred years and more,
> Waited without a suitor till he came.
>
> .   .   .   .
>
> So that when Mary still remained below
> She mounted up with Christ upon the cross!
> But that too darkly I may not proceed,
> Francis and Poverty for these two lovers
> Take thou henceforward in my speech diffuse.
> Their concord and their joyous semblances
> The love, the wonder, and the sweet regard,
> They made to be the cause of holy thoughts.

Francis and Poverty — these lovers seem
strange indeed to twentieth-century eyes. An age
when philanthropy strives for the abolition of
poverty and invites enlightened self-interest to its
aid cannot readily understand one who welcomed
poverty as a blessed condition. "No man," said a

disciple of St. Francis, " was ever so covetous of wealth as he of poverty."

We hear St. Francis discoursing with brother Leo concerning perfect bliss. It lies not in knowledge or power or even in the ability to convert the infidels to the Holy Faith. " When we shall come to St. Mary of the Angels dripping with rain and tormented with cold and hunger, and we shall knock at the door, and the porter shall say, ' Who are ye ? ' and we shall answer, ' We are your brethren,' and he shall say, ' You lie, you are two knaves that go about deceiving the people and stealing from the poor ' — if, when he leaves us in the cold and wet we shall patiently endure, and say within ourselves, ' Perhaps the porter reads us aright,' then, O brother Leo, thou mayest say, ' Herein lies perfect bliss.' "

We hear the passionate prayer, " O Lord Jesus, point out to me the ways of poverty which were so dear to thee. O Jesus, who chosest to be poor, the favor I ask of thee is to give me the privilege of poverty and to be enriched by thy blessing."

This was not the temper of ordinary asceticism. St. Francis was in temper more an Epicurean than a Stoic. He was a lover of pleasure and was not

content with any kind of pleasure short of what
he conceived to be the highest. The ascetic was
interested primarily in the salvation of his own
soul. Wealth and comfort were the temptations
of the devil to cheat him of his future reward.
The hermit accepted poverty as the hard road to
Heaven; to St. Francis it was Heaven itself.

" Property is robbery," he would have said, but
not in the sense in which a modern communist
would use the words. It is the robbery not of
one's neighbor but of one's self. We take for
granted that wealth is a good thing and poverty
an evil. No, St. Francis would say, there is no
good thing but what is good for the soul. It is
good to be humble, sympathetic, and thankful.
It is good to be conscious of God's presence
everywhere and to be close to the lowliest of his
creatures. The means of this grace are nearer to
the peasant than to the prince. There are some
things that wealth buys. The rich man has his
comforts, his sheltered home, his group of friends
and dependents, his servants and his wide estates;
his is the meekness that inherits the earth.

St. Francis found joy in the sacrifices and austerities which to others were so painful. The pre-

dominant note is that of gladness. In the midst
of his penances he is light-hearted. He interpreted
more literally than we do the words, " Take no
thought for the morrow." Some things are possible in Umbria and Galilee that seem wildly im-
practicable under the fickle skies of New England.
The sober prose of religion may be translated into
all languages and verified by all human experience, but there is an idyllic poetry of religion that
belongs only to the climate where that poetry
had birth. "The Little Flowers of St. Francis"
grew out of the same kindly soil and under the
same friendly skies that nourished the lilies that
Jesus loved.

St. Francis always wore his halo with an easy
grace. In spite of his scourgings and fastings he
was blithe and debonair. He was saint-errant, as
full of romance as any knight-errant of them all.
He was a lover of spiritual adventure, and delighted to attempt the impossible.

To St. Francis voluntary poverty meant spiritual freedom. The preacher was no longer dependent on powerful patrons or rich parishioners
or even on the fickle multitudes. The missionary
did not need a missionary board. He did not

have to wait for a church building to be erected and a pulpit to be prepared. Even a hermitage was a superfluity. "The true hermit," said St. Francis, "carries his cell about with him." And so he and his disciples preached and asked no man's leave. Through all the byways of Italy they wandered, proclaiming that God was in the fields as well as in the churches. Entering a village Brother Francis would say, "Love God and repent, good people. Love God and do penance." And Brother Egidio would say, "Yes, good people, do as Brother Francis says, for he says what is right."

And if there were no people to preach to there were always our sisters, the birds, and now and then there was a wicked wolf who would yield to moral suasion. We smile at this way of preaching to every creature, but it is as we smile at the idiosyncrasies of one we love.

Many a preacher who has confined his preaching to human kind has put less good sense into his sermons and shown less insight into the causes of sin than did Francis in his discourse to the wolf of Gubbio. The inhabitants who had suffered from his depredations hated him for his

wolfish iniquities. The saint saw that the cause
of the evil was economic rather than moral. He
was a right-minded wolf; the trouble was that he
was hungry. St. Francis entered into a covenant
of peace with him.

" 'Brother Wolf, inasmuch as it pleases you to
make and keep this peace, I promise you that so
long as you shall live you shall not suffer hunger,
forasmuch as I am aware that hunger has caused
your every crime. But since I have got for you
this grace, I require, Brother Wolf, your promise
never again to do harm to any human being,
neither to any beast. Do you promise?' And
St. Francis stretching forth his hand, the wolf
uplifted his right paw and gave him the pledge
of faith as best he could."

It was in the same spirit that St. Francis
went forth on his mission to the Sultan. The
Crusaders had gone forth to destroy the infidels.
Francis, in the simplicity of his heart, thought the
better way would be to convert them. Neither
way proved to be altogether effective, but certainly the latter plan was the more Christian.

In the history of preaching there have been
many vicissitudes. Sometimes the preacher has

been a philosopher, sometimes an advocate, sometimes he has adopted the tone of a man of business. In the preaching of St. Francis we are taken
back to the time of the wandering minstrels.

"So great was the sweetness and consolation
of his spirit that he called for Brother Pacificus
whom the world entitled the King of Verse and
Courteous Doctor of Song, and desired to send
him with the other friars to go together through
the world, preaching and singing the "Praises of
the Lord." And he desired that he among them
who was the best preacher should first preach to
the people, and when the sermon was ended all
the others should sing together the "Praises of the
Lord," as the Lord's minstrels; and at the end
he desired the preacher should say to the people,
'We are the Lord's minstrels, and the reward we
ask of you is that you turn to true repentance.'"

No wonder that the people loved Brother Francis when he brought religion to them in such a
fashion, and that there would gather around him

> A crowd of shepherds with as sunburnt looks
> As may be read of in Arcadian books.

With all his saintly austerities St. Francis
was always a gentleman. Even the most admir-

ing biographers cannot hide his humanness. The
Lives of the Saints do not contain many such
incidents as that in the chapter in " The Mirror
of Perfection " entitled " How he comforted a
Sick Friar by eating Grapes with Him." It was a
little thing to do, but I am sure that St. Dominic
would never have thought of it. The friar had
been overdoing the mortification of the flesh, and
had fallen ill. " Blessed Francis said to himself:
' If that friar would eat ripe grapes in the morning I believe he would be cured! And as he
thought so he did. Rising early in the morning,
he called the friar secretly, and took him to a
vineyard near the place, and choosing a vine that
had good grapes fit for eating, he sat down by the
vine with the friar and began to eat grapes, that
the friar should not be ashamed of eating alone.
. . . And all the days of his life this friar remembered the pity and compassion shown him by the
blessed Father, and would relate what had happened to the other friars."

It was an age of miracles, but St. Francis never
allowed them to clutter up his little world. They
must keep their place. When Brother Peter died
in great sanctity, he was immediately worshiped

as a saint. Great crowds came to his tomb, and
many miracles were wrought. This was well, but
there must be a measure in all things. So one day
St. Francis went to the door of the tomb, and his
most persuasive voice said, " Brother Peter, in
your lifetime you gave perfect obedience. Know
that your brethren are disturbed by the crowds
that come to your tomb. I command you, by
holy obedience, that you work no more miracles."
And from that day Brother Peter abstained from
any interference with the order of nature.

A true son of the Church, yet because of the
unworldliness of his nature Francis from the first
transcended the sphere of ecclesiasticism, and lived
in the freedom of the spirit. In an age when ritu-
alism was triumphant he chose an unsacerdotal
ministry. At a time when the highest piety was
supposed to manifest itself in the building and
adornment of churches, he insisted on the higher
grace of charity. When a case of need was presented to him, he said : " Sell the ornaments on
the altar of the Blessed Virgin. Be assured that
she would be more pleased to have her altar without adornment than to see the gospel of her Son
any longer set at naught."

Pope Innocent had many who came with ambitious plans. There were always monks who desired to be abbots, and priests who desired to be bishops. But one day Brother Francis came desiring that he and certain poor brethren might be allowed to live according to the rule of the gospel. They were not content to be poor after the conventional fashion of the great monastic institutions, where corporate wealth was married to individual poverty. Their poverty should be real. Almost everything had been organized around a treasury. They would like to organize brotherly kindness, patience, humility, and love according to their own laws.

And the request was made so simply that Pope Innocent could do nothing but grant it, though it made his own ambitions stand out in startling contrast.

The life of St. Francis was very mediæval, which was but another way of saying that its idealism was not balanced by the scientific temper. Men in those days delighted in paradoxes, and were contented with no half measures. His experience was different from ours. He did not

confront the poverty of the slums of our great
cities. It was the poverty of Umbria. It was a
poverty that was acquainted with hunger and
which wore coarse garments, but it had the freedom of the fields and the open roads. We
have problems to solve with which he was un-
acquainted.

Yet there is something in his daring paradox
which attracts us. Beneath all its extravagance
there is a vitality in the joyous worship of My
Lady Poverty. For what is worship? It is, literally, worth-ship. It is the recognition of intrin-
sic values. It is just here that the modern man is
beginning to be distrustful of himself. He has
been marvelously successful in obtaining his desires, but has he desired the best things? In the
height of his achievement he cannot help asking,
"After all, is it worth what it has cost?"

Things turn out differently from what had been
expected. A life devoted to personal gain is
likely to be disappointing. A whole community
which has no other means of estimating worth
than the increase in wealth is still more disappointing. It has no proper means of government.
A plutocracy is but another name for moral an-

archy. Special interests become intolerably dom-
ineering and override the common good. In a
society where everything is measured by money,
where is the limitation to despotism? What
is to prevent the rich man from buying up his
neighbors and using all their talents to serve his
own narrow purposes? He is able to pay for the
best food and drink and shelter. Why may he
not bend to his will the best human ability?

The answer comes from the iconoclasts, who
strike boldly at the idols of the market-place.
They have something that is not for sale, and they
can afford to laugh at the highest bidders. They
are not asking favors. They are likely to be in-
experienced in the ways of the world, but the
world fears them as it fears all forces which it
cannot understand. They cannot be cajoled or
threatened, for they have learned that it is possible
to be happy and poor.

My Lady Poverty has still her worshipers.
She has long been honored by the devotion of
true artists. The man of science gravely acknow-
ledges her, and confesses without shame that he is
too busy to make money. There are statesmen
who are the despair of the party managers because

when the question comes, "What can we do for you?" they answer "Nothing." Every now and then there occurs that disconcerting phenomenon which we call genius. It upsets all calculations and refuses to respond to the law of supply and demand. The second best may be bought, but the very best is given away. Now and then, too, out of our conventional gentilities there comes an ideal gentleman. He would adorn the most exclusive circles, were it not that he has a passion for the best society, and he has learned that the best society is never exclusive. He takes the part of the uttermost man, and finds his joy in the companionship of those who are aspiring and struggling. And there is the increasing number of the nature-lovers who enter into the religious feelings which St. Francis voiced in "The Song of the Creatures." They love one who could worship out of doors, and speak familiarly of Master Sun and Brother Wind and Sister Water. As they sit around their campfires they join heartily in the praise of Brother Fire. "He is jocund, robust, and strong and bright."

They love to read again the story of how St. Francis and Brother Masseo stopped at noon under a tree where there was a broad smooth stone to serve as a table for their simple meal. Close by was a spring of cold water.

" What a treasure we have here!" cried Francis in delight.

" Father," answered Brother Masseo, " how can you talk so when we have no tablecloth or knife or cup!"

Brother Masseo voices the opinion of the majority, but there are increasing numbers of true Franciscans. St. Francis is the patron saint of those who believe in Nature as well as in Grace. In spite of all his austerities he is endeared to us because he represented the bohemianism of piety.

AS HE SEES HIMSELF

ᴥᴥ

THE exercises of Commencement Day had
been unusually interesting, though prolonged. I had attended them all. I had listened
to the wisdom of the selected members of the
graduating class, and afterwards to the less dignified but more optimistic remarks of the old grad-
uates. The general impression that I received
was that though the country had been in danger,
the worst was over.

Returning home I found a caller waiting for me
in the library. He was a rather handsome man in
his way, but a close observer might have noticed
a certain shiftiness in his eyes and hard lines about
his mouth, and perhaps other signs of a misspent
life. Not being a close observer, I did not notice
any of these things. He struck me as an ordinary
person with whom it might be a pleasure to talk.
I was somewhat surprised at his first remark,
which was made by way of introduction.

" I am," he said, " well known to the police, and am said to be the most dangerous criminal of my class now at large. I am an expert forger and have served time in four prisons."

His frank statement was preliminary to the request for a temporary loan that would enable him to complete the work of reformation, that was endangered by a lack of funds. It was late in the day, and before acceding to his request it was necessary that there should be some investigation, so I asked him to call on the morrow.

" I have been at the Commencement exercises all day," I said, " and am not in a condition to be of much help to you just now; but if you would like to stay a while and chat, I should be glad."

He welcomed the suggestion, and, now that the matter of business had been postponed, he was at his ease. In a friendly way he made me acquainted with the general theory of forging and check-raising, — at least so far as it is intelligible to the lay mind. His criticism of prison management was acute, and he pointed out the seamy side of the plans of the reformers. I listened with docility to his story of the under world. He was a well-educated man with an appreciation of good literature, which was a characteristic, he informed me, of most forgers. He was especially interested in sociology, and had all its best phrases at his tongue's end. He attributed all his misfortunes to Society. For one thing I listened in vain, — the admission that in some respects he might himself have been remiss. The idea of reciprocal obligation did not seem to have any place in his philosophy. As delicately as I could I tried to turn the conversation from the sin of Society, which I readily acknowledged, to the less obvious point of personal responsibility. Granting that Society was imperfectly organized, that juries were ignorant, and judges lacking in the quality of mercy, and prison wardens harsh, and chaplains too simple-minded, were there not faults on the other side that it might be profitable to correct? It was of no use to try to induce such currents of thought; they were quickly short-circuited.

At last I said, "You have told me what you did before you concluded to reform. I am curious to know how, in those days, you looked at things. Was there anything which you would n't have done, not because you were afraid of the law, but because you felt it would be wrong?"

"Yes," he said, "there is one thing I never would do, because it always seemed low down. I never would steal."

It was evident that further discussion would be unprofitable without definition of terms. I found that by stealing he meant petty larceny, which he abhorred. In our condemnation of the sneak thief and the pickpocket we were on common ground. His feeling of reprobation was, if anything, more intense than that which I felt at the time. He alluded to the umbrellas and other portable articles he had noticed in the hallway. Any one who would take advantage of an unsuspecting householder by purloining such things was a degenerate. He had no dealings with such moral imbeciles.

It seemed to me that I might press the analogy which instantly occurred to me between "stealing" and forgery.

"Do they not," I said, "seem to you to amount to very much the same thing?"

I had struck a wrong note. Analogies are ticklish things to handle, for things which are alike in certain respects are apt to be quite different in other respects. His mind was intent on the differences. The sneak thief, he told me, is a vulgar fellow of no education. The forger and the check-raiser are experts. They are playing a game. Their wits are pitted against the wits of the men who are paid high salaries for detecting them. They belong to quite different spheres. If we are looking for analogies we should look up and not down.

"You wanted to know," he said, "what was the difference between stealing and check-raising. Now, let me ask you a question. What's the difference between check-raising and some of those big financial operations we 've all been reading about? Suppose I have a check for five dollars, and I put my brains into it and I manipulate it so that I can pass it off for five hundred. I shove it in to the cashier and he takes it. Before he finds out his mistake, I have made myself scarce. What's the difference between that transaction and what the 'big fellows' on the street are doing?" He mentioned several names that I had not thought of in that connection.

"The difference," said I, "is — " Then it occurred to me that it was a subject to which I should give further thought. So we postponed

the conversation till he should call again —
which he never did.

I may be doing injustice to my friend the
forger, but he gave me the impression that he
considered himself to be, on the whole, a rather
admirable character.   His proposed change of
business seemed to be rather a concession to the
prejudices of the legal profession than the result
of any personal scruple. As he saw himself
he was a man of idealistic temper whose ideals
conflicted with social usage.   Society was all the
time getting into his way, and in the inevitable
collisions he had usually the worst of it. He
regretted this, but he bore no malice. By the
time a man has reached middle life and accumulated a good deal of experience he takes the world
as he finds it.

He had encased himself in a moral system
which was self-consistent and which explained to
his own satisfaction all that had happened to him.
One thing fitted into another, and there was no
room for self-reproach.

Many attempts have been made to depict the

character of an accomplished scamp. But Gil Blas and Roderick Random and Jonathan Wild the Great are after all seen from the outside. The author may attempt to do them justice, but there is a vein of irony that reveals a judgment of his own. They lack the essential element of incorrigibility, which is that the scamp does not suspect himself, has not found himself out.

No novelist has ever been able to give such a portraiture of a complacent criminal as was given a century ago in the autobiography of Stephen Burroughs.

Burroughs was the son of a worthy clergyman of Hanover, New Hampshire, and from the outset was looked upon as a black sheep. As a mere boy he ran away from home and joined the army, and then with equal irresponsibility deserted. He became a ship's surgeon, a privateersman, then a self-ordained minister, a counterfeiter, a teacher of youth, a founder of libraries, and a miscellaneous philanthropist. He was a patriot and an optimist and an enthusiastic worker in the cause of general education. He was chock-full of fine sentiment and had a gift for its expression. He enjoyed doing good, though in his own way, and never neglected any opportunity to rebuke those who he felt were in the wrong. He had a desire to reform the world, and had no doubt of the plans which he elaborated. He was capable on occasions of acts of magnanimity, which, while not appreciated by the public, gave him great pleasure in the retrospect. The intervals between his various enterprises were spent in New England jails. These experiences only deepened his love of liberty, which was one of the passions of his life.

Burroughs had a happy disposition that enabled him to get a measure of satisfaction out of all the vicissitudes of his life. He had learned neither to worry nor to repine. He was not troubled by the harsh judgments of his fellow men, for he had learned to find his happiness in the approbation of his own conscience.

He writes: "I possess an uncommon share of sensibility, and at the same time maintain an equality of mind that is uncommon, particularly in the midst of those occurrences which are calculated to wound the feelings. I have learned fortitude in the school of adversity. In draining the cup of bitterness to its dregs, I have been taught to despise the occurrences of misfortune.

This one thing I fully believe, that our happiness is more in our power than is generally thought, or at least we have the ability of preventing that misery which is so common to unfortunate situations. No state or condition in life, but from which we may (if we exercise that reason which the God of Nature has given us) draw comfort and happiness. We are too apt to be governed by the opinions of others, and if they think our circumstances unhappy, to consider them so ourselves, and of course make them so. The state of mind is the only criterion of happiness or misery."

It was from this lofty point of view that Stephen Burroughs wrote the history of his own life. His tendency to didacticism interferes with the limpid flow of the narrative. Sometimes a whole chapter will be given over to moralizings, but the observations are never painful. They all reveal the author's cheerful acquiescence in the inevitability of his own actions. Along with this there is the air of chastened surprise over the fact that he was made the object of persecution.

At the very beginning of the narrative one recognizes an independence which would do credit to a better man. In New England, clergymen have always been looked upon as making good ancestors, and Burroughs might have been pardoned if he had shown some family pride. From this weakness he was free. " I am," he says, " the only son of a clergyman, living in Hanover, in the State of New Hampshire; and were any to expect merit from their parentage, I might justly look for that merit. But I am so far a Republican that I consider a man's merit to rest entirely with himself, without any regard to family, blood, or connection."

The accounts of the escapades of his boyhood are intermingled with dissertations on the education of youth. " I have been in the habit of educating youth for seven years, constantly; in the course of my business I have endeavored to study the operations of the human heart, that I might be able to afford that instruction which would be salutary; and in this I find one truth clearly established, viz.: a child will endeavor to be what you make him think mankind in general are."

The neglect of this truth on the part of his parents and teachers was the cause of much annoyance to Burroughs. Throughout his life he was the innocent victim of an educational mistake.

Though after a while he learned to forgive the early injustice, one can see that it rankled. He endeavored to think well of mankind in general, but it was more difficult than if he had been habituated to the exercise in infancy.

At Dartmouth young Burroughs was peculiarly unfortunate; he fell into bad company. As an unkind fate would have it, his room-mate was an exemplary young man who was studying for the ministry. It appears that this misguided youth attempted to entice him into what he describes as "a sour, morose, and misanthropic line of conduct." Nothing could have been more disastrous. " To be an inmate with such a character, you will readily conceive, no way comported with a disposition like mine, and consequently we never enjoyed that union and harmony of feeling in our intercourse as room-mates which was necessary for the enjoyment of social life."

To the malign influence of his priggish room-mate several misfortunes were attributed. In endeavoring to restore the moral equilibrium which had been disturbed by the too great scrupulosity of his chum, he exerted too much strength in the other direction. The result was that "a powerful triumvirate" was formed against him in the Faculty. The triumvirate triumphed and his connection with Dartmouth ended suddenly.

This gave occasion to a chapter on the failure of the institutions of learning to prepare for real life. The author declares "more than one half of the time spent in the universities, according to their present establishment on this continent, is thrown away, and that my position is founded in fact I will endeavor to prove."

I do not see how his argument is affected by the fact to which the editor calls attention in a carping footnote. " It is not strange that the author should reason in this manner. He was expelled from college in the second quarter of his second year, and in fact he studied but little while he was a member." The editor, I fear, had a narrow mind and judged according to an academic standard which Burroughs would have despised.

From the uncongenial limitations of a college town it was a satisfaction to escape to sea. Here Burroughs's versatility stood him in good stead. " Having no doctor engaged, I undertook to act in that capacity; and after obtaining the assistance, advice, and direction of an old practitioner, together with marks set on each parcel of medicine, I thought myself tolerably well qualified to perform the office of a physician on board the ship."

From his seafaring life Burroughs returned with his reputation under a cloud. There were ugly rumors afloat which were readily believed by a censorious world. For once he confesses that his philosophy failed him. " I returned to my father's house sunken and discouraged; the world appeared a gloomy chaos; the sun arose to cast a sickly glimmer on surrounding objects; the flowers of the field insulted my feelings with their gayety and splendor; the frolicsome lamb, the playful kitten, and the antic colt were beheld with those painful emotions which are beyond description. Shall all nature, shall the brute creation break out into irregular transports, by the overflowing of pleasing sensations, whilst I am shut out from even the dim rays of hope ? "

Certainly not. To a mind constituted as was his there was an absurdity in the very suggestion. The brute creation should not have any monopoly of comfortable sensations, so he cheered up immediately and spent the next year loafing around his father's house.

He had been on the coast of Africa and had taken part in some strange scenes, but his moral sense had not been blunted to such an extent that he could not grieve over some infractions of the moral law which he observed in peaceful Hanover. He regretted that he had been led inadvertently by a young man named Huntington to join a party which robbed a farmer's beehive.

"For some unaccountable reason or other, youth are carried away with false notions of right and wrong. I know, for instance, that Huntington possessed those principles of integrity that no consideration would have induced him to deprive another of any species of property, except fruit, bees, pigs, and poultry. And why it is considered by youth that depriving another of these articles is less criminal than stealing any other kind of property, I cannot tell."

Burroughs himself was inclined to take a harsher view of these transgressions than he did of some others; for example, of counterfeiting, in which he was afterwards for a time engaged during one of his brief pastorates.

The argument by which his scruples in this particular were overcome are worth repeating. The law was indeed violated in its letter, but might not a justification be found by one who interpreted it in a large spirit of charity?

"Money is of itself of consequence only as we annex to it a nominal value as the representation of property. Therefore we find the only thing necessary to make a matter valuable is to induce the world to deem it so; and let that esteem be raised by any means whatever, yet the value is the same, and no one becomes injured by receiving it at the valuation."

The principle of fiat money having been established, the only question that remained was whether the circumstances of the times were such as to justify him in issuing the fiat. The answer was in the affirmative. "That an undue scarcity of cash now prevails is a truth too obvious for me to attempt to prove. Hence whoever contributes to increase the quantity of cash does not only himself but likewise the community an essential benefit."

It was in his attempt to benefit the community in this way that he first experienced the ingratitude of republics, being landed in the Northampton jail.

But to see Burroughs at his best one must enter into his thoughts at that crisis in his life when he determined that his true vocation was preaching. He lingers fondly on his emotions at that period. It was at a time when he had been driven out of Hanover for conduct which had outraged the feelings of that long-suffering community.

"One pistareen was all the ready cash I had on hand, and the suddenness with which I departed deprived me of the chance to raise more. Traveling on leisurely I had time for reflection."

As was usually the case when he reflected, he grew more serene and enjoyed a frame of mind that bordered on the heroic.

"I began to look about me to see what was to be done in my present situation and to what business I could turn my attention. The practice of law, which would have been most to my mind, I could not undertake until I had spent some time in the study, which would have been attended with expense far beyond my abilities; therefore this object must be laid aside. Physic was under the same embarrassments; business in the mercantile line I could not pursue for want of capital.

. . . What can be done? There is one thing, said contrivance, that you can do, and it will answer your purpose — preach."

The idea came to him as an inspiration, but immediately there was suggested an objection which to a less resourceful mind would have seemed insuperable. " What an appearance should I make in my present dress? which consisted of a light gray coat, with silver-plated buttons, green vest, and red velvet breeches."

Down the Connecticut valley he trudged, calling to mind his father's old sermons and gradually working himself into a state of pious rapture. The heart of no young pulpiteer beat with more appropriate emotions than his, when on the next Sunday, under an assumed name, he preached his first sermon in the village of Ludlow. " I awoke with anxious palpitation for the issue of the day. I considered this as the most important scene of my life — that, in a great measure, my future happiness or wretchedness depended on my conduct this day. The time for assembling approached! I saw the people come together. My feelings were up in arms against me, my heart would almost leap into my mouth. What a strange thing, said I, is man! Why am I thus perturbated by these whimsical feelings!"

The moment he began the service these perturbations came to an end. Words came in a steady flow, and he felt sure that he had found his true calling in life. "No monarch when seated on a throne had more sensible feelings of prosperity than what I experienced at this time."

The neighboring town of Pelham being without a minister, Burroughs presented himself as a candidate, and was enthusiastically accepted. He made a specialty of funeral sermons, and was soon in demand in all the surrounding country. It was at this time also that he became acquainted with the coiner who showed him how he might surreptitiously increase the amount of cash in circulation. All went well till an enemy appeared who called him by name and revealed his antecedents. All Pelham was in an uproar, for the Pelhamites were "a people generally possessing violent passions, which, once disturbed, raged uncontrolled by the dictates of reason, unpolished in their manners, possessing a jealous disposition, and either very friendly or very inimical, not knowing a medium between these extremes."

In this case they suddenly became very inimical, and Burroughs was again compelled to depart under cover of darkness. His night thoughts
were always among his very best.

"Journeying on, I had time for reflection. At
the dead of night — all alone — reflection would
have its operation. A very singular scene have I
now passed through, said I, and to what does it
amount? Have I acted with propriety as a man,
or have I deviated from the path of rectitude? I
have had an unheard-of, disagreeable part to act;
I do not feel entirely satisfied with myself in this
business, and yet I do not know how I could have
done otherwise, and have made the matter better.
My situation has been such that I have violated
the principle of veracity which we implicitly
pledge ourselves to maintain towards each other,
as a general thing, in society. Whether my peculiar circumstances would warrant such a line of
procedure is the question. I know many things
will be said in favor of it as well as against it."

From this difficult question of casuistry he
found relief in reverting to the one instance in
which he had been clearly wrong, viz., joining
the young men in Hanover in their raid on the

farmer's beehive. " My giving countenance to an open breach of the laws of the land in the case of the bees was a matter in which I was justly reprehensible; but that matter is now past. I must take things as they are, and under these circumstances do the best I can. I know the world will blame me, but I wish to justify my conduct to myself, let the world think what it may."

In this endeavor he was highly successful; and as he walked on, his spirits rose. He contrasted his own clear views with the muddled ideas of his late parishioners. " They understand the matter in the gross, that I have preached under a fictitious name and character, and consequently have roused many ideas in the minds of the people not founded on fact. Therefore they concluded from this general view the whole to be founded on wrong. The name impostor is therefore easily fixed on my character. An impostor, we generally conceive, puts on feigned appearances in order to enrich or aggrandize himself to the damage of others. That this is not the case with me in this transaction, I think is clear. That I have aimed at nothing but the bare necessaries of life, is a fact."

Having thus cleared himself of the charge of imposture, he determined to rest his case on the broad ground of religious liberty. " That I have a good and equitable right to preach, if I choose and others choose to hear me, is a truth of which I entertain no doubt."

When he was pursued into the borders of the town of Rutland, it was too much for his patience. "I turned and ran about twenty rods down a small hill, and the Pelhamites all after me, hallooing with all their might, 'Stop him! stop him!' To be pursued like a thief, an object of universal speculation to the inhabitants of Rutland, gave me very disagreeable sensations, which I determined not to bear. I therefore stopped, took up a stone, and declared that the first who should approach me I would kill on the spot. To hear such language and to see such a state of determined defiance in one whom they had lately reverenced as a clergyman struck even the people of Pelham with astonishment and fear."

By the way, there follows a scene which makes us suspect that parts of Massachusetts in the good old days may have had a touch of "the wild West." The two deacons who were leaders of the

mob drew attention to the fact that besides having come to them under false pretenses Burroughs
had absconded with five dollars that had been ad-
vanced on his salary. He owed them one sermon
which was theirs of right. In the present excited
state of public opinion it was obviously impossible for Burroughs to deliver the sermon, but it
was suggested that he might give an equivalent. A peacemaker intervened, saying, " Wood
keeps an excellent tavern hard by; I propose
for all to move up there." This proposal was
accepted by all. " I therefore came down, and we
all went up towards the tavern. I called for drink,
according to the orator's advice, to the satisfaction of all."

After that the career of Burroughs went on
from bad to worse, but never was he without the
inner consolations that belong to those who are
misunderstood by the world. Even when he un-
successfully sought to set fire to the jail he was
full of fine sentiments borrowed from Young's
"Night Thoughts." He quotes the whole passage
beginning

Night, sable goddess ! from her ebon throne.

This he seems to consider to be in some way a

justification for his action. He is ever of the opinion that a man's heart can not be wrong so long as he is able to quote poetry.

The various incarcerations to which he was subjected might only have imbittered a less magnanimous mind. They rather instilled into Burroughs a missionary spirit. He felt that he ought to take more pains to enlighten the ignorance of the world in regard to his excellent qualities. "I have many times lamented my want of patient perseverance in endeavoring to convince my persecutors of their wrong by the cool dictates of reason. Error once seen ought to be corrected. The pruning hook should never be laid aside; then we should live up to the condition of our nature, which requires a state of improving and progressing in knowledge till time shall cease."

But even Burroughs was human. It is easier to bear great misfortunes than to meet the petty annoyances of every-day life. To one who plans his life in such a way as to depend largely on the casual gifts of strangers, their dilatoriness is often a cause of real anxiety.

Here is a painful incident which happened to him in Philadelphia. He applied to a member of

Congress for a small sum of money. The gentleman was not all that he should have been. " The
most striking features of his character were his
great fondness for close metaphysical reasoning
and a habit of great economy in his domestic
concerns, and he had so long practiced upon this
system that any variation from it in a person's
conduct or any want of success in a person's
undertakings were, in his view, perfectly wrong.
This was the man to whom I applied as my ulti-
matum."

We can see at a glance that such a man was
likely to be disappointing.

"I described my circumstances to him in as clear
terms as possible, and afterwards told him of the
request I wished to make. Without giving me an
answer either in the affirmative or the negative,
he went on with a lengthy discourse to prove that
my system of economy had been wrong, drawing
a comparison between his prosperity and my adversity, and then pointed out a certain line of conduct that I ought then to take up and observe,
and offered to assist me in prosecuting such; but
as his plan had many things in it which I could
not reconcile my mind to, I took the liberty of

reasoning with him upon a better plan which I had marked out in my own mind."

Upon this, the congressman became obstinate and would do nothing. His depravity came to Burroughs as a sudden shock.

" When I took a view of the world, of the pomp and splendor which surrounded crowds which perpetually passed before my eyes, to see them roll in affluence and luxury, inhabiting lofty houses, with superb equipages, and feasting upon all the delicacies of life, under these affluent circumstances withholding from me what would never have been missed from their superfluity, this brought to my mind a train of ideas that were desperate and horrid. . . . My eyes lighted up with indignation, my countenance was fortified with despair, my heart was swollen to that bigness which was almost too large for my breast to contain. Under this situation I arose with a tranquil horror, composedly took my hat, and politely bid Mr. Niles farewell. I believe the desperate emotions of my heart were apparently manifested to his view by my countenance; his apparent immovability relaxed, he put his hand in his pocket, and handed me three dollars. This act of kindness in a moment melted the ferocious feelings of my heart, all those desperate sensations vanished, and I found myself a man."

Dear reader, have you not often taken a part in such a scene? When instead of handing out your dollars at once you conditioned them upon adherence to some " line of conduct," — your conscience accuses you that you might have pointed even to the buck-saw, — do you realize what a pitiful spectacle you made of yourself?

Stephen Burroughs does not at all fulfill our preconceived notion of an habitual criminal. He did not love evil for its own sake. His crimes were incidental, and he mentions them only as the unfortunate results of circumstances beyond his own control. His life was rather spent in the contemplation of virtue. There were some virtues which came easy to him, and he made the most of them. Like an expert prestidigitator, he kept the attention fixed on what was irrelevant, so that what was really going on passed unnoticed. He had eliminated personal responsibility from his scheme of things, and then proceeded as if nothing were lacking. He had one invariable measure for

right and wrong. That was right which minis-
tered to his own peace of body and of mind; that
was wrong which did otherwise.

We are coming to see that that imperturb-
able egotism is the characteristic of the "criminal
mind" that is least susceptible to treatment. Sins
of passion are often repented of as soon as they
are committed. Sins of ignorance are cured by
letting in the light. Sins of weakness yield to an
improved environment. But what are you going
to do with the man who is incapable of seeing
that he is in the wrong? Treat him with compassion, and he accepts the kindness as a tribute
to his own merits; attempt to punish him, and he
is a martyr; reason with him, and his controversial
ardor is aroused in defense of his favorite thesis.

Sometimes the lover of humanity, after he has
tried everything which he can think of to make
an impression on such a character and to bring
him to a realizing sense of social responsibility,
becomes utterly discouraged. He feels tempted
to give up trying any longer. In this he is wrong.
He should not allow himself to be discouraged.
Something must be done, even though nobody
knows what it is.

But if the lover of humanity *should* give up for a time and take a rest by turning his attention to a more hopeful case, I should not be too hard on him. My Pardoner, I am sure, must have some indulgence for such a weakness.

A MAN UNDER ENCHANTMENT

❧

"I SAT down by the wayside of life like a man under enchantment." So Nathaniel Hawthorne wrote of his own visionary youth, and, truth to tell, the spell lasted through life.

The wayside itself was not conducive to dreams. It was a busy thoroughfare. Eager traffickers jostled one another, and there was much crying up of new wares. Many important personages went noisily along. There was a fresh interest in all sorts of good works and many improvements on the roadway. There were not many priests or Levites passing by on the other side, for ecclesiasticism was not in fashion, but there were multitudes of Good Samaritans, each one intent on his own brand-new device for universal helpfulness. There were so many of them that the poor man who fell among philanthropists often sighed for the tender mercies of the thieves. The thieves, at least, when they had done their work would let him alone. From time to time there would come groups of eager reformers, advance agents of the millennium. At last there came down the road troops hurrying to the front, and there was the distant sound of battle.

It was a stirring time, the noon of the nineteenth century; and the stir was nowhere more felt than in New England. It was a ferment of speculation, a whirl of passion, a time of great aspiration and of no mean achievement.

But if you would get a sense of all this, do not turn to the pages of Nathaniel Hawthorne. The ardor of Transcendentalism, the new spirit of reform, the war between the States, — these were noted, but they made no very vivid impression on the man who sat under enchantment. There was an interval between these happenings and his consciousness that made them seem scarcely contemporaneous.

It is a fashion in literary criticism to explain an author by his environment. With Hawthorne this method is not successful. It is not that his environment was not interesting in itself. His genius was essentially aloof. It was a plant that drew its nourishment from the air rather than from the soil. There are some men who have the happy faculty of making themselves at home wherever they happen to be. Hawthorne, wherever he had been born, would have looked upon the scene with something of a stranger's eye. Indeed, when we think about it, the wonder is that most of us are able to take the world in such a matter-of-fact way. One would suppose that we had always been here, instead of being transient guests who cannot even engage our rooms a day in advance.

It is perhaps a happy limitation which makes us to forget our slight tenure, and to feel an absolute ownership in the present moment. We are satisfied with the passing experience because it appears to us as permanent.

To the man who sat by the wayside the present moment did not stand in the sunshine sufficient unto itself. It did not appear, as it did to the man of affairs, an ultimate and satisfying reality. He was not unobservant. He saw the persons passing by. But each one, in the present moment, seemed but a fugitive escaping from the past into the future. Futile flight! unavailing freedom! for in the Future the Past stands waiting for it. As he looked at each successive action it was as one who watches the moving shadow of an old deed, which now for some creature has become doom.

Did I say that Hawthorne was little influenced by his environment? It would be truer to say that the environment to which he responded was that to which most men are so strangely oblivious. He felt what another Salem mystic has expressed:

> Around us ever lies the enchanted land
> In marvels rich to thine own sons displayed.

The true-born Yankee has always persisted, in spite of the purists, in using " I guess " as equivalent to " I think." To his shrewd good-humored curiosity, all thinking resolves itself into a kind of guesswork; and one man has as good a right to his guess as another.

It is a far cry from the talk of the village store to Emerson and Hawthorne, but to these New Englanders thinking was still a kind of guessing. The observer looks at the outward show of things, which has such an air of finality, and says, " I guess there's something behind all this. I guess it's worth while to look into it."

Such a mind is not deterred by the warnings of formal logic that there is "no thoroughfare." When it leaves the public road and sees the sign

"Private way, dangerous passing," it says, "that looks interesting. I guess I'll take that."

And from our streets and shops and newspapers, from our laboratories and lecture rooms and bureaus of statistics, it is, after all, such a little way to the border-land of mystery, where all minds are on an equality and where the wisest can but dimly guess the riddles that are propounded.

Hawthorne belonged to no school or party. To the men of his generation he was like the minister of whom he writes who preached with a veil over his face.

Nor is his relation in thought to his ancestry more intimate than that to his contemporaries. Born to the family of New England Puritanism, we think we recognize the family likeness — and yet we are not quite sure. There are traits that suggest a spiritual changeling.

When we enter into the realm of Hawthorne's imagination we are conscious of sombre realities.

Is not this a survival of the puritanic spirit, with its brooding mysticism, its retributive predestination, its sense of the judgment to come? It was said of Carlyle that he was a Calvinist who had lost his creed. May not the same be said of Hawthorne? The old New England theology had in him become attenuated to a mere film, but through it all may we not see the old New England conscience?

Doubtless there is much of this transmitted influence. Hawthorne himself insisted upon it. Speaking of "the stern and black-browed Puritan ancestors," he said, "Let them scorn me as they will, strong traits of their nature have intertwined themselves with mine."

But it is possible to exaggerate such likenesses. In Hawthorne's case there is danger of argument in a circle. We say that there is something in Hawthorne's imagination, in its sombre mysticism, in its brooding sense of destiny, which is like that of the spirit of the inhabitants of Salem and Boston in the old days when they walked through the narrow streets and through the shadowy woodland ways pondering the fatal sequences of life.

But how do we see these old Puritans? We see them through Hawthorne's eyes. His imagination peoples for us the old houses. Was Hawthorne's genius tinged with Puritanism, or are our conceptions of the Puritan character largely Hawthornesque? It is not necessary to argue this matter; it might be better to answer "Yes" to both questions.

It is the privilege of a creative genius to imprint his own features upon his forbears. It is difficult here to determine which is cause and which is effect. How marvelously Rembrandt gets the spirit of the Dutch Burgomeisters! It was fortunate for him that he had such subjects, — stalwart men with faces that caught the light so marvelously. Yes, but had it not been for Rembrandt, who would have told us that these Dutch gentlemen were so picturesque?

The subject of a good artist is accurately figured; the subject of a great artist is transfigured. We cannot separate the historic reality from the transfiguring light.

But however Hawthorne may have been influenced by his Puritan inheritance, it would be hard to find one whose habitual point of view was further removed from what we are accustomed to call the "New England conscience." It is the characteristic of that type of conscience that it has an ever-present and sometimes oppressive sense of personal responsibility. It is militant and practical rather than mystical. To it evil is not something to be endured but something to be resisted. If there is a wrong it must be righted, and with as little delay as possible.

The highest praise a Puritan could give his pastor was that he was " a painful preacher." Jonathan Mitchell, writing of the beginnings of the church in Cambridge, says that the people of Cambridge " were a gracious, savory-spirited people, principled by Mr. Sheperd, liking an humbling, heart-breaking ministry and spirit."

The Puritan theology was based on predestination, but the Puritan temper was not fatalistic. When that latter-day Puritan, Lyman Beecher, was expounding the doctrines of the divine decrees, one of his sons asked him, " Father, what if we are decreed to be lost ? " The answer was, " Fight the decrees, my boy ! "

The Calvinistic spirit was exactly opposite to the fatalistic acquiescence which shifts the responsibility from the creature to the Creator. To be sure the fall of man took place a long time ago, but we cannot say that it was none of our business. It was not an hereditary misfortune to be borne with fortitude; it was to be assumed as our personal guilt. "Original sin" means real sin. Adam sinned as the typical and representative man, and every man became a sinner. No individual could plead an *alibi*. The "conviction of sin" was not the acquiescence in a penalty, — it was the heartbreaking consciousness of the "exceeding sinfulness of sin."

"In Adam's fall *we* sinned all." When they said that, they were thinking not of Adam, but of themselves. *They* did it; it was the guilt that was imputed to them. Sensitive consciences were tortured in the attempt fully to realize their guilt.

The real inheritors of this type of conscience were to be found among many of the radical reformers and agitators who were Hawthorne's contemporaries and with whom he had little in common. When their formal creed had fallen off, there remained the sense of personal guilt for original sin. The sin of the nation and of the whole social order weighed heavily upon them and tortured them, and they found relief only in action.

All this was foreign to Hawthorne's mind. In his treatment of sin there is always a sense of moral detachment. We are not made to see, as George Eliot makes us see, the struggle with temptation, — the soul, like a wild thing, seeing the tempting bait and drawing nearer to the trap. Hawthorne begins after the deed is done. He shows us the

wild thing taken in a trap
Which sees the trapper coming thro' the wood.

Of what is the trap made? It is made of a deed already done. Whence comes the ghostly trapper? He is no stranger in the wood. There is no staying his advance as he makes his fatal rounds.

In the preface to the "House of the Seven Gables" the author gives the argument of the story, — "the truth, namely, that the wrong-doing of one generation lives into the successive ones, and, divesting itself of every temporary advantage, becomes a pure and uncontrollable mischief."

This is the theme of the Greek tragedy — Nemesis. The deed is done and cannot be undone; the inevitable consequences must be endured.

In the "Scarlet Letter," when Hester and Roger Chillingworth review the past and peer into the future, Hester says, "I said but now that there can be no good event for him or thee or me who are wandering together in this gloomy maze of evil, and stumbling at every step over the guilt wherewith we have strewn our path."

But is the present stumbling guilt or is it merely misery? The old man replies, "By the first slip awry thou didst plant the germ of evil, but since that moment it has been a dark necessity. Ye that have wronged me are not sinful, save in a kind of typical illusion, neither am I fiend-like who have snatched a fiend's office from his hands. It is our fate. Let the black flower blossom as it may."

Strange words to come from one who had sat in a Puritan meeting-house! It is such comment as the Greek Chorus might make watching the unfolding of the doom of the house of Agamemnon. And when the tale of the "Scarlet Letter" has been told, how does the author himself look upon it? How does he distribute praise and blame?

"To all these shadowy beings so long our near acquaintances — as well Roger Chillingworth as his companions — we would fain be merciful. It is a curious subject of observation and inquiry whether love and hatred be not the same thing at bottom. Each in its utmost development supposes a high degree of intimacy and heart-knowledge; each renders one individual dependent for his spiritual life on another; each leaves the passionate lover or the no less passionate hater forlorn and desolate by the withdrawal of its subject. Philosophically considered, therefore, the passions seem essentially the same except that one happens to be seen in celestial radiance and the other in a dusky lurid glow." This is not the Puritan Conscience uttering itself. It is an illusive and questioning spirit.

If in his attitude toward human destiny Hawthorne was in some essential respects un-Puritan, so also was he un-modern. There is a characteristic difference between antique and modern symbols for those necessary processes, beyond the sphere of our own wills, by which our lives are determined. The ancients pictured it with austere simplicity. Life is a simple thread. The Fates spin it. It is drawn out on the distaff and cut off by the fatal shears.

Compare this with the phrase Carlyle loved to

quote, " the roaring loom of Time." Life is not a
spinning-wheel, but a loom. A million shuttles
fly; a million threads are inextricably interwoven.
You cannot long trace the single thread; you
can discern only the growing pattern. There is
inevitable causation, but it is not simple but complex. The situation at the present moment is the
result not of one cause but of innumerable causes,
and it is in turn the cause of results that are
equally incalculable. We are a part of

> the web of being blindly wove
> By man and beast and air and sea.

Men of science show us how the whole acts upon
each part and each part acts upon the whole.
Modern novelists attempt, not always successfully, to give the impression of the amazing complexity of actual life, where all sorts of things are
going on at the same time.

Whether we look upon it as his limitation or
as his good fortune, Hawthorne adhered to the
spinning-wheel rather than the loom. We see the
antique Fates drawing out the thread. A long
series of events follow one another from a single
cause.

A part of the power of Hawthorne over our

imagination lies in his singleness of purpose. In "The Marble Faun" we are told, "The stream of Miriam's trouble kept its way through this flood of human life, and neither mingled with it nor was turned aside."

We are made to see the dark streams that do not mingle nor turn aside, and we watch their fatal flow.

But is this real, normal life? In such life do not the streams mingle? Are not evil influences quickly neutralized, as noxious germs die in the sunshine? No one would more readily acknowledge this than Hawthorne. He says: "It is not, I apprehend, a healthy kind of mental occupation to devote ourselves too exclusively to the study of individual men and women. If the person under examination be one's self, the result is pretty certain to be diseased action of the heart almost before we can snatch a second glance. Or if we take the freedom to put a friend under the microscope, we thereby insulate him from many of his true relations, magnify his peculiarities, inevitably tear him into parts, and of course patch him clumsily together again. What wonder, then, that we be frightened at such a monster, which, after all — though we can point to every feature of his deformity in the real personage — may be said to have been created mainly by ourselves."

The critic of Hawthorne could not describe better the limitation of his stories as pictures of real life. His characters, however clearly conceived, are insulated from many of their real relations, and their peculiarities are magnified.

In the preface to " The Scarlet Letter " he says that the tale " wears to my eye a stern and sombre aspect, too much ungladdened by the tender and familiar influences which soften almost every scene of Nature and real life, and which undoubtedly should soften every picture of them."

One who would defend Hawthorne the Author against Hawthorne the Critic must point out the kind of literature to which his work belongs. When we judge it by the rule of the romance or of the realistic novel, we fail to do justice to its essential quality. The romancer, the story-teller pure and simple, is attracted by the swift sequence of events. His nimble fancy follows a plot as a kitten follows a string. Now it happens that in a world constituted as ours is the sequence of events follows a moral order. A good story has always

in it an element of poetic justice. But the romancer does not tell his story for the sake of the
moral. He professes to be as much surprised
when it is discovered as is the most innocent
reader. In like manner the realistic novel, in proportion as it is a faithful portrayal of life, has an
ethical lesson. But the writer disclaims any purpose of teaching it. His business is to tell what
the world is like. He leaves the rest to your intelligence.

But there is another kind of literature; it is
essentially allegory. The allegorist takes a naked
truth and clothes it with the garments of the imagination. Frequently the clothes do not fit and
the poor truth wanders about awkwardly, self-
conscious to the last degree. But if the artist be
a genius the abstract thought becomes a person.

Hawthorne's work is something more than allegory, but his mind worked allegorically. His
characters were abstract before they became concrete. He was not a realist aiming to give a com-
prehensive survey of the actual world. He con-
sciously selected the incidents and scenes which
would illustrate his theme.

In his conclusion of " The Marble Faun," when

the actors have withdrawn, the Author comes before the curtain and says that he designed " the story and the characters to bear, of course, a cer-tain relation to human nature and human life, but still to be so artfully and airily removed from our mundane sphere that some laws and proprieties of their own should be implicitly and insensibly acknowledged. The idea of the modern Faun, for example, loses all the poetry and beauty which the Author fancied in it and becomes nothing better than a grotesque absurdity if we bring it into the actual light of day." This is not realism.

It is a mood in which the bounds between ro-mance and allegory fade away; persons become symbols and symbols have breathed into them the breath of life. The story and the truth it shadows are one.

The mood is common in poetry. Poets like Dante and Spenser and Shelley from it have given us

> Wise and lovely songs
> Of fate and God and chance and chaos old,
> And love.

There is a point where " dreams begin to feel the truth and stir of day," where the incidents of existence assume a dream-like character, and where dreams become transparent symbols of reality. There are moods in which our familiar world seems strange to us, and we walk in it as on some bewildered shore.

In such moods to meet Hawthorne is a great experience. He is no longer shy and aloof, but he opens to us his heart, and with friendly zeal points out each object of interest — for in this border-land he is at home.

THE CRUELTY OF GOOD PEOPLE

❧

THE cruelty of bad people is easily explained. They are cruel because they enjoy watching the pain of others. There are also the ignorant and half-formed, to whom the word "inhumanity" applies literally. They have not yet been really humanized. Before they can habitually yield to feelings of compassion there is much to be done in developing their higher natures. They must be urged to

> Move upward, working out the beast,
> And let the ape and tiger die.

The beast has a long start, and the ape and tiger die hard.

But this is only half the story. We are continually surprised at the cruelty that is possible in those in whom there seems to be no tigerish survival. It is intimately associated with the higher rather than with the lower part of the nature. It is spiritual, rational, and moral. The cruelty of

women and priests is proverbial — and they are
good women and good priests.

Listen to the talk in a drawing-room when some
question involving the fate of thousands is introduced. There is a strike or lock-out. It means that
the hostile parties are struggling on a narrow ledge
between two precipices. The workmen are trying
to push the employers into the abyss of bank-
ruptcy; the employers are exerting every means
in their power to hurl their antagonists into the
abyss of starvation. It is a battle to the death, and
in many a home pale-faced women are watching
it with despairing eyes. But what says my lady
who likes to talk about current events? It is
evident when she begins to speak that she is not
touched by the tragedy of it all. Nero watching
the burning of Rome could not assume an air of
more complete detachment. She talks as if it were
nothing to her. Or the talk turns to the affairs of
state. Issues that involve the fate of nations awake
in her only a languid curiosity. The diplomacy
of prudent statesmen who are endeavoring to
keep the peace strikes her as mere dilly-dallying.
She wants to see something doing. She enjoys a
romantic sensation, and urges on those who would

give her this pleasure. Was there ever a useless war without fair faces looking down upon it approvingly — at least at the beginning ?

> I saw pale kings, and princes too,
> Pale warriors, death pale were they all;
> They cried, "La Belle Dame sans Merci
> Hath thee in thrall."

Yet she who in regard to the great affairs which involve millions may appear as "La Belle Dame sans Merci" may be to all those whom she knows a minister of purest kindness. It is only towards those whom she does not know that she is pitiless.

Philosophers are usually cruel in their judgments of the persons and events of the passing day, and that is perhaps the reason why no nation has been willing to take the hint from Plato and allow the philosophers to rule. It would be too harsh a despotism. Flesh and blood could not endure it. For the philosopher is concerned with general laws and is intolerant of exceptions, while it is the quality of mercy to treat each person as in some degree an exception. Fancy the misery that would be involved in the attempt to level us all up to the cold heights of abstract virtue on which Spinoza dwelt. One shudders to think of the calamity that would ensue were all our lawmakers to be suddenly Hegelianized. All the attempts to alleviate the hard conditions under which people are living would cease. The energy that is now spent in trying to abolish abuses would then be directed toward explaining them. What wailings would go up from earth's millions on the proclamation of the rule of un-limited Spencerianism! We should look back with envy to the good old times of Nero and Tamerlane.

As the Inquisition handed its victims over to the secular arm and disclaimed all further responsi-bility, so this new tyrant would hand over all the unfit to the unobstructed working of natural law. No attention would be paid to our senti-mental preferences for particular persons. Those merciful interferences which have been the con-trivance of mankind for the protection of weak-ness must be swept aside. The unfit must take the full penalty justly visited on their unfitness. The moment we begin to particularize we rebel. Pity revolts against a too cold philosophy.

It is needless to say that the theologians have often attained refinements of cruelty unknown even to the most severely logical of the secular philosophers. They have been able to distill out of the purest religious affections a poison capable of producing in the sensitive soul unutterable agony. Then they have watched the writhing of the victim with a cold benevolence. The worst of it was that the benevolence was real in spite of the fact that it froze all the fountains of natural pity.

Jonathan Edwards was not merely a good man in the ordinary sense. His goodness rose into ideal heights. He had a genius for ethics as well as for religion. He is still a teacher of teachers. But this wonderful man, who must ever have a high place among the leaders and inspirers of mankind, has an equally high place among the torturers of the spirit. To understand the kind of pain which he inflicted we must not be content with the threatenings of torment in sermons like that on "Sinners in the Hands of an Angry God." The pictorial imagery which now startles us was common enough in his day. The torments of sinners was an ordinary theme; Edwards added

appreciably to the torments of the saints. His
vivisection of the human soul was without compunction. In the hearts and desires of the innocent he discovered guilt for which there was no
pardon. Every resting-place for natural human
affection was torn away, and when at last from
the clear heaven the love of God shone down in
dazzling splendor, it shone upon a desert.

The cruelty of it all is seen in its effects on
minds naturally prone to melancholy. Read the
journal of a disciple of Edwards, David Brainerd,
and remember that for several generations that
journal was esteemed a proper book to put into
the hands of youth. The editor of the Journal
says, " As an example of a mind tremulously ap-
prehensive of sin, loathing it in every form and
for its own sake, avoiding even the appearance
of evil, rising above all terrestrial considerations,
advancing rapidly in holiness, and finding its only
enjoyment in the glory of God, probably no similar work in any language can furnish a parallel."
Poor Brainerd ! Every step along the heavenly
way cost him a pang. He never could forget for
more than a few hours at a time that he was human, and to be human was to be vile. The groans

follow one another with monotonous iteration. He loved God, but he felt his guilt in not loving him more. He was not only afraid of hell, but of a heaven of which he was unworthy.

"I seem to be declining with respect to my life and warmth in divine things. I deserve hell every day for not loving my Lord more. . . . I saw myself very mean and vile, and wondered at those who showed me respect."

We all feel that way sometimes, but to have the feelings set down day by day for years at a time seems hardly profitable. We are relieved when occasionally the editor summarizes the spiritual conflicts of a week or two without going into details, as in the latter part of December, 1744. "The next twelve days he was for the most part extremely dejected, discouraged and distressed, and was evidently much under the power of melancholy. There are from day to day most bitter complaints of exceeding vileness, ignorance, and corruption; an amazing load of guilt, unworthiness even to creep on God's earth, everlasting uselessness, fitness for nothing, etc., and sometimes expressions even of horror at the thoughts of ever preaching again. But yet in this time of dejection he speaks of several intervals of divine help and comfort."

The pitiful thing about it all was that Brainerd's distress arose not from the consciousness of any particular shortcoming of his own, which after all was finite. He was endeavoring to realize the meaning of that infinite guilt which was his as a child of Adam. That guilt must be infinite because it was a sin against infinite purity and power. When he had repented to the very utmost of his ability, he was conscious that he had not repented enough.

When he went to New Jersey as a missionary to the Indians, it was this abnormal spiritual sensitiveness which he endeavored to impart to the aboriginal mind.

He found it difficult to bring the Indians to that degree of spiritual anguish which, in his view, was necessary to their salvation. He could make them understand the meaning of actual transgression, but they were dull of comprehension when he urged them to repent of original sin.

"Another difficulty," he says, "which I am now upon, is that it is next to impossible to bring them to a rational conviction that they are sinners by nature, and that their hearts are corrupt and sinful, unless one can charge them with some gross act of immorality such as the *light of nature* condemns."

One would suppose that the missionary might have found among his untutored Indians enough actual transgressions to have brought to them a conviction of sin and a desire for a better life. But no, that was not enough, it would have fallen far short of what he had in mind. It would have only convinced them that they were sinners individually considered, and would not have overwhelmed them with the guilt of the race. So he hit upon a device to turn their minds from the incidental trangressions of mature life to the central fact that depravity was innate and universal.

" The method which I take to convince them that we are sinners by nature is to lead them to an observation of their little children: how they will appear in a rage, fight and strike their mothers before they are able to speak or walk, while they are so young that they are incapable of learning such practices. . . . As children have never learned these things, they must have been in their natures;

and consequently they must be allowed to be by nature the children of wrath."

It did not seem to occur to Brainerd that in thus setting the child in the midst of them as an illustration of the kingdom of wrath he was not imitating the method of Jesus. Even in his treatment of the sins of later life there is something illustrative of the cruel system which dominated him.

"I then mention all the vices I know the Indians to be guilty of, and so make use of these sinful *streams* to convince them that the *fountain* is corrupt. This is the end for which I mention their wicked practices to them; not because I expect to bring them to an effectual reformation merely by inveighing against their immoralities, but hoping that they may hereby be convinced of the corruption of their hearts, and awakened to a sense of the depravity and misery of their fallen state."

Brainerd had in mind a profound truth; every great moral awakening is accompanied by pain. But he was not content with that which comes naturally. All specific reformation in morals and manners was subordinated to that which he conceived to be the essential thing,—that they should feel to its full extent the misery of being human.

In every readjustment of thought or advance in the manner of life there is involved a vast amount of unescapable pain. There is also a great deal of pain that is gratuitously inflicted. In the contest between the forces of conservatism and progress it is difficult to say which side is more open to the charge of cruelty.

In reading history our sympathies are usually with the bold innovator. He stands alone against the world and proclaims an unpopular truth. He is misunderstood, reviled, persecuted for right-eousness' sake. The defenders of the old order are hard-hearted persecutors who hound him to death.

But this is only half the story. A glimpse of the other side is given in the very term we use. We speak of the *defenders* of the old order. We only understand their feelings when we remem-ber that they were really on the defensive. The things they held most sacred were attacked by a ruthless power which they could not understand. They flew to the rescue of sanctuaries about to be violated. They often fought as those in mortal agony, using blindly such weapons as came to their hands.

In " The Faerie Queene" Una, the fair symbol of Truth, wanders through the forest protected by her lion. He is a good lion and faithful to his lady.

> The lyon would not leave her desolate,
> But with her went along, as a strong gard
> Of her chast person, and a faythfull mate
> Of her sad troubles and misfortunes hard :
> Still when she slept, he kept both watch and ward ;
> And when she wakt, he wayted diligent
> With humble service to her will prepard ;
> From her fayre eyes he took commandëment
> And ever by her lookes conceived her intent.

That is the picture that comes to the adherent of the old order. The pure virgin Truth walked unharmed, with her strong protector by her side. At length a proud Paynim attacked the gentle lady. Then it was that

> her fiers servant, full of kingly aw
> And high disdaine, whenas his soveraine Dame
> So rudely handled by her foe he saw,
> With gaping jawes full greedy at him came,
> And, ramping on his shield, did weene the same
> Have reft away with his sharp rending clawes.

But it was a losing battle. The lion's sudden fierceness was all in vain.

> O then, too weake and feeble was the forse
> Of salvage beast.

Now that her defender is slain, what is to become of Lady Truth?

> Who now is left to keepe the forlorn maid
> From raging spoile of lawless victor's will?

The lover of the old order does not stop to ask whether the lion may not have made a mistake, and whether the object of his attack may not have been, instead of a proud Paynim, only a Christian knight who had approached to ask his way. Nor does he feel pity for the pains inflicted by the lion's "sharp rending clawes." He only cries, "Poor lion! Poor Lady Truth!"

"But," says the careful reader, "are you not getting away from your subject? You proposed the question, 'Why are good people so cruel?' You began with the conversation of excellent ladies in the drawing-room, and now you have wandered off into faery land, and are talking about the Lady Truth and the noble lion who died in her defense. I fear you are losing your way."

On the contrary, dear reader, I think, as the children say when they are hunting the thimble, we are " getting warm." We started out to find a cause for the obliviousness of good people to the pain which they inflict on others, and we have come into the region of allegory. Now, one of the chief reasons why good people are cruel is that it is so easy for them to allegorize.

In an allegory virtues and vices are personified. Each is complete in itself, and when it once has been set going it follows a preordained course. It does not grow into something else, and it is in-capable of repentance or improvement. In the morality plays a virtue is as virtuous and a vice as vicious at the beginning as at the end. Spenser prefixes to " The Faerie Queene " a prose explan-ation of the meaning of each important character. " The first of the Knight of the Red-crosse, in whom I set forth Holynes; the second of Sir Guyon, in whome I sette forth Temperance ; the third of Britomartis, a lady knight, in whom I picture Chastity." Now, after this explanation we are relieved of all those anxieties which beset us when we watch creatures of flesh and blood set-ting out in the world to try their souls. Everything is as much a matter of invariable law as the reactions of chemical elements. The Knight of the Red-cross may appear to be tempted, but he is really immune. He cannot fall from grace. From that disaster he is protected by the definition. We have only to learn what the word holiness means to know what he will do. As for Sir Guyon, when once we learn that he is Temperance, we would trust him anywhere. For such characters there is nothing possible but ultimate triumph over their foes. And what of their foes? Being allegorical characters, they cannot be reformed. There is nothing to do but to kill them without compunction, or if we can catch them in the traps which they have set for others, and make them suffer the torments they have themselves invented, so much the better. We welcome the knight —

> Who slayes the Gyaunt, wounds the Beast,
> And strips Duessa quight.

We have no compunctions as we watch the administration of poetical justice. Whatever happens to the false Duessa and to such miscreants as Sansfoy and Sansjoy and Sansloy, we say that it serves them right.

If we can only hold fast to the allegorical clue, and be assured that he is dealing with sins and not with persons, we can follow Dante through purgatory without flinching. The moral always is a good one, and full of suggestiveness.

But the moment we mistake an allegorical character for a person of flesh and blood we get into trouble. Even the most perfect parable represents only a certain phase of reality. When it is forced beyond its real intention and taken literally it shocks our sense of humanity. It needs to be interpreted by the same wise spirit that conceived it. We repeat the story of the symbolic virgins who had forgotten to put oil in their lamps, or of the servant who was too timid to put his master's money out to usury. The child asks, " Was n't it cruel of those wise virgins not to give the others just a little of their oil? And after the door was shut and the foolish virgins knew how foolish they were and were sorry, could n't the people inside have opened the door just a little bit? And just because the servant was afraid to go to the bank with the money, because it was so little, ought the master to have been so hard with him as to say, 'Cast ye the unprofitable servant

into the outer darkness; there shall be weeping
and wailing and gnashing of teeth?' Why did n't
he give him another chance?"

Then the parent will explain that these are
symbolic characters. Or perhaps he may not try
to explain, but change the subject and read a
story of real people like that of the prodigal son
or the good Samaritan. The child may be made
to understand that while the door is always shut
against a sin, it is always open for the sinner who
repents.

The sensitive child takes up the "Pilgrim's Progress" and reads of the way Christian went on his
way to the heavenly city, meeting all kinds of
people, yet apparently without sympathy for most
of them. "Why did he leave his wife and little
children in the City of Destruction and go off
alone? If he knew that the city was to be burned
up, why did n't he stay with them? He does n't
seem to care very much for what happens to
people who are not of his set." So it seems to be.
Mr. Hold-the-world, Mr. Money-love, and Mr.
Save-all walk along with him, and then they go
off the path to look into a silver-mine. Christian
does n't take the trouble to find out what became

of them. Bunyan says coolly, " Whether they fell into the pit by looking over the brink or whether they went down to dig, or whether they were smothered by the damps that commonly arise, of these things I am not certain; but this I observed, that they were never seen that way again." Christian goes on after the tragedy perfectly unconcerned, singing a cheerful hymn. It was none of his business what happened to those who wandered off the road. He is rather pleased than otherwise when Vain-Confidence falls into the pit. When "the brisk young lad," Ignorance, joins him Christian converses with him only long enough to find out his name and where he came from. Then instead of trying to improve him he leaves him behind. Poor Ignorance trudges after, but he never can catch up.

All this is right in an allegory. Ignorance must be left behind, Vain-Confidence must perish in the pit; from the City of Destruction we must flee without waiting for others to follow. This is a very simple lesson in the way of life. The next lesson is more difficult and it is quite different, — how to treat ignorant and vainglorious and otherwise imperfect *persons.*

The first thing we have to remember is that they are persons, and that persons are quite different from allegorical characters. Persons can change their minds, they can repent and aspire after a better life, and above all they have feelings, — which abstract virtues and vices do not have. Does not the cruelty of the good chiefly arise from the fact that they do not see all this?

In a preceding essay we have considered Hawthorne's judgment on the characters which he himself created. His most powerful story of sin and retribution wears to his eyes " a stern and sombre aspect too much ungladdened by the tender and familiar influences which soften almost every scene of Nature and real life." He was aware that he was depicting not all of life, but only one aspect of it. He saw the characters of the " Scarlet Letter," as they saw themselves, " in a kind of typical illusion." He was fully aware that his treatment was symbolic rather than realistic. Real life is infinitely more complex and therefore more full of possibilities of good than any symbolic representation of it.

I do not think that good people are really as cruel at heart as one would be led to think from

their words, or even from their acts. I remember
a good professor of theology who was discoursing
on the way in which the Canaanites were destroyed
in order that Israel might possess the land.

"Professor," asked a literal-minded student,
"why did the Lord create the Canaanites, any-
how ? "

"The Lord created the Canaanites," answered
the professor, " in order that Israel might have
something on which to whet his sword."

The words were bloodthirsty enough; and yet
had I been a Canaanite in distress I should have
made my way at once to the good professor's
house. I am sure that the moment he saw me he
would have taken me in and ministered tenderly
to my distresses and protected me from an un-
kindly world. But I should have taken the pre-
caution to let him see me before he learned my
name. A Canaanite in the abstract would be an
abomination to him, and I would have to take
pains to make him understand that I was a human being.

The word "cruel " is in its derivation akin to
" crude; " it is that which is raw and unripe. Like
all other good things, righteousness at first is

crude. Crude righteousness takes no account of the difference between a sinner and his sin; it hates both alike with a bitter hatred, and visits on each the same condemnation. It is harsh and bitter. For all that it is a good thing, this unripe fruit of righteousness. Give it time and sunshine, and it will grow sweet and mellow.